Stonefield Stories

By Sheila Hébert

This book is lovingly dedicated to my parents,
Dorothy and Bill Harkness.

Table of Contents

Preface

In the early 1940's, news reports about the war raging in Europe were so alarming that my parents thought it would be a good idea to buy a house in the country in case they had to flee falling bombs or an enemy invasion. Dad wanted a property with enough room to keep a cow, raise some chickens and grow vegetables. Mum just wanted to find a place so quiet and out of the way that an invading army would march right past and falling bombs would not be a threat.

They found their bolt-hole quite by chance in a tiny hamlet halfway between Montreal and Ottawa. A crooked, weather-beaten signpost whispered, rather than announced that they had come to Stonefield. As they continued their way along the gravel road, they saw several fields that were stony indeed, and along a strip of friendlier terrain they counted seven houses. At the crossroads they turned a corner and discovered a quaint ivy-covered hotel, a general store with a wide verandah across the front and a very large horse barn. The most impressive feature of the place was Lock number 5 of the Grenville Canal. They parked the car and walked over to take a closer look at the canal which stretched peacefully as far as the eye could see in either direction.

It was when they turned around to go back to their car that they spied a little peak-roofed house tucked cozily behind the general store and facing the canal. There was a 'For Sale' sign nailed to the gate so they decided to take a closer look. The house listed a bit to one side and more than a few windowpanes were cracked. Several of the shingles on the roof were gone altogether and the whole place was in desperate need of a coat of paint. Some people would have called it downright shabby but Mum and Dad told each other the place had character.

Mum was delighted by the vine covered porch at the front of the house and Dad was pleased to see a shed-cum-summer kitchen at the back. An apple tree shaded the living-room window, raspberry canes straggled along one side of the yard and a neglected garden plot stretched across the back of the property. A well-worn path led from the back door to an outhouse which was nicely screened from view by a generous planting of hollyhocks. There was ample room on the far side of the house to build a little stable and a henhouse. The only running water was a creek that gurgled past the dining-room window and the lighting system consisted of oil lamps and candles. In other words, it was perfect for their requirements, so before the day was out, they bought it.

While Mum and Dad waited for the war to go one way or the other, they decided to use the house as a summer home. My sister Diane was 5 years old and I was 2 when we moved in. Mum and Dad invited their best friends, Polly and Len to join us. Their son, Ross was 6 and their daughter, Cheryl was 3 and we all got on like a house on fire. The people of Stonefield welcomed us into their homes and their hearts like long-lost relatives. By the time the war ended, our summers in Stonefield were so firmly woven into the fabric of our lives that we carried on for another 15 years, moving in joyfully every June and going back to the city with great reluctance every September.

The stable and henhouse never did get built but over the years, Mum and Aunt Polly tamed the garden and wall-papered every room in the house. Dad and Uncle Len pruned trees, cut back hedges and kept our beloved old house in good repair with a lot of ingenuity and very little money.

All of us picked the berries that grew in the surrounding countryside and Mum and Aunt Polly made enough jam to keep us dreaming of Stonefield throughout the winter. We kids flew out the door in the morning in search of adventure and usually found it. We followed the farmers to the fields at haying time, swam in the canal every day and only wore shoes when we had to.

We thought those happy times would never end but in 1958 the construction of a hydro-electric dam in the Ottawa River not far from Stonefield began. Over the next few years, the residents were forced to leave the homes and farms that had sheltered and fed them for generations. We scattered to the four winds ahead of the rising water that eventually washed Stonefield right off the map.

The pain of separation was terrible. For many years that pain was all I remembered when I thought about Stonefield. But with time comes healing, so now I can write about those precious days when it seemed that the sun shone all day and the rain only fell at night, when our parents shrugged off the cares of city living and we children lived and played in Heaven.

Some of the stories that follow are recounted exactly as I remember them, while others have been embroidered with the threads of my imagination. There are even a few that seemed to flow from my pen of their own accord. I leave it to you to decide which is which.

Chapter 1

Uncle Bertie Helps Out

For our neighbors on Moffat Avenue in Verdun, the 24th of May week-end was the time to celebrate Queen Victoria's birthday. Most people hung out their Union Jacks on the Friday night and had fish and chips for supper. Others raised a glass or two on Saturday night and sang a few choruses of 'There'll Always Be an England'. Everyone flocked to the band concert in the park on Sunday after lunch and stayed until dark to enjoy the fireworks display. Fathers snoozed on Monday afternoon, mothers organized bridge games and kids played 'Kick the Can' in the lane.

But our family was different. For us, the 24th of May week-end was the time when we opened our cottage and got it ready for the coming summer. Union Jacks, band concerts and a day off didn't enter into it. My sister Diane and I kept well out of the way of our parents while they worked like Trojans for the entire week-end, cleaning and repairing whatever damage had been done during the past winter. The only break Mum and Dad got was the forty winks they snatched out on the lawn on Monday afternoon before packing up to drive back to the city.

One year, Dad's youngest brother Bertie came along to help out and what happened that 24ᵗʰ of May week-end is permanently engraved in my mind. Talk about fireworks!

On Friday night, Diane raised her glass and intoned, "Here's to Queen Victoria. May she rest in peace, and here's to Lockside Cottage, the best summer house in the whole world."

On Saturday morning, we helped our parents load the car with suitcases, groceries, assorted mops, brooms and buckets. When we drove past the park we paid no attention to the firemen who were setting up the launching site for the fireworks. We didn't give the bandstand so much as a glance either. We only had eyes for the road that would lead us to the country.

Our parents weren't quite as happy as we were. Their tempers flared even before we got to the corner of the street.

"I bet you forgot the vinegar," said Mum accusingly, "The windows will be covered with flyspecks and cobwebs."

"What do you take me for?" Dad snapped, "I showed you the list before we packed everything. You put the vinegar in the box yourself."

"I have too many things to remember," Mum grumbled, "It's no joke keeping track of two households. Sometimes I wonder if it wouldn't be easier to stay in the city."

Diane and I decided it would be best to say nothing so we played several silent games of tic-tac-toe to pass the time. Fortunately our parents' irritation lessened with every passing mile and they were smiling and happy by the time we got to Stonefield.

Diane and I flew into the house as soon as Dad got the door open. We scampered excitedly from room to room, climbing up the stairs and sliding down the bannister over and over again. Mum opened the downstairs windows and threw back the shutters to let in the warm air, while Dad went upstairs to inspect the ceilings for patches of damp.

"Looks like the roof hasn't leaked this year," he reported, sounding very relieved.

After that he put a shovel into the wheelbarrow and went to the end of the garden to clean out the outhouse. Diane and I always knew how he felt about his chores because he whistled, 'I'm Forever Blowing Bubbles' for the ones he didn't mind doing and 'Rock of Ages' for the ones he disliked. Dealing with the outhouse was good for several renditions of 'Rock of Ages'.

Mum began by checking the condition of the pantry, gingerly looking for evidence of mice. Then she shivered her way upstairs to shake the eiderdowns out of their long sleep. She draped them across the windowsills to warm up before dusting the bedroom furniture and sweeping the floors. Mum didn't whistle like Dad but we knew how she felt about her chores because she talked to herself as she worked.

When we heard something along the lines of, "My goodness, I'd forgotten just how pretty these pillowcases are," or "Oh good, this blanket'll do for another summer," then we knew all was well. But if we heard screams or appeals for divine intervention, we knew that she had discovered something dreadful and quite possibly dead. That's when she would threaten to drop everything and go back to the city. Diane and I were terrified when that happened.

So you can imagine our panic that day when she cried, "Oh, my sainted aunt! This is more than flesh and blood can stand. I've a good mind to go back to the city this minute!"

Diane grabbed my arm and squeaked, "Did you hear that? The city. What'll we do?"

I shrugged miserably. Tears rolled down my cheeks.

But luckily that year, we had Uncle Bertie with us to lighten the atmosphere and the work load, so when he spied Diane and me weeping at the foot of the stairs, he winked and said confidently, "Don't you worry about a thing. Your mum'll settle down. After all, I'm here to help and I can turn my hand to anything. Once the work's done everything will be fine. Why don't you go outside and play for a while?"

Reassured, Diane and I went off to explore our favourite haunts. We climbed the apple tree, took turns on the swing and dabbled our toes in the creek. Completely relaxed, we sauntered back to the house. Uncle Bertie was mopping the kitchen floor and humming tunelessly to himself. Dad was washing windows and whistling 'I'm Forever Blowing Bubbles', but to our dismay, Mum was still complaining bitterly.

"It's as cold as the grave in here," she muttered as she pounded lumpy mattresses and punched clammy pillows, "And Lord have mercy," she squealed, "What's that under the wardrobe?"

"Mum doesn't sound too happy," I gabbled to Uncle Bertie, "We better do something quick. Any minute now she's going to take us back to the city."

Uncle Bertie said soothingly, "All your mum needs is a nice cup of tea and a bit of heat upstairs. I'll get the fire going. That should do the trick. Could you get me the matches and some wood?"

We flew to the woodshed. I grabbed the matches and some kindling. Diane picked up two logs and we hurried back to the kitchen.

Uncle Bertie was peering into the depths of the stove and muttering to himself, "Look at that. There's a few twigs in there already and bits of straw mixed up with what looks like feathers. That's funny. Well, never mind. It'll all burn nicely."

Suddenly Mum squawked. Diane and I froze and stared at one another. What was it this time? A nest of mice in the blanket box? Raccoons in the chimney cupboard?

Thinking quickly, Diane cupped her hands around her mouth and shouted up the stairs, "Mum, we're making tea. It'll be ready in a minute and we'll bring it up."

Lowering her voice to a whisper she urged me, "Get a cup and saucer and rattle them around so she hears. We've got to get her mind off things."

I sure didn't want Mum to talk about going back to the city so I hopped to it. I polished the prettiest cup and saucer in the dresser and rummaged around until I found the jug with pink roses all around the rim. In the meantime Diane dug into the box of groceries to find the biscuits.

"Get the kettle, Sheila, and we'll fill it up at the pump," Diane said. As we were going out the back door I asked Uncle Bertie how the fire was coming along.

"Well, it seems a little slow. Probably the wood was a bit damp," he said.

Diane and I exchanged uneasy glances. Uncle Bertie understood. He wiggled his bushy eyebrows and rolled his bright blue eyes at us, "Cheer up, you two, I'll have the fire positively blazing by the time you're back with the water."

But it wasn't blazing. It wasn't even flickering and Uncle Bertie looked puzzled.

"I don't know what the trouble is," he said, " I twisted the paper good and tight, put the kindling on top and lit it before I dropped the logs in, but the stove doesn't seem to be drawing the way it should."

"Try the bellows. Sometimes that helps," Diane suggested.

Overhead we heard Mum talking crossly to herself, "Dratted squirrels. I'm sure they've built a nest in the attic. Could be an army of them up there for all I know."

We cringed as she screeched shrilly, "Ye gods! A bat! Go on, get out, you miserable flea bitten creature. Get out! Oh my, sometimes I hate the country."

We jumped like scared rabbits when she slammed the window down with a crash.

We looked pleadingly at Uncle Bertie.

"Hurry up or we're gonna end up back in the city," we urged him.

"Ok, Ok, keep your hair on," he said. He poked the tip of the bellows deep into the fire-box and gave a mighty squeeze. A few puffs of smoke drifted upwards.

"Once more for luck, eh girls?" he asked with a cocky grin. He opened the bellows and squeezed again. We edged closer to see what was happening.

"It worked, it worked," we cried as bright flames began to lick at the logs, "You did it, Uncle Bertie."

"Course I did, nothing to it!" he said proudly.

He replaced the stove lid and gave us a wink. The crackling noise got louder. The kettle began to hiss. I spooned tea leaves into the pot and Diane poured some milk into the jug. Uncle Bertie grinned at us and wiggled his eyebrows like a pair of caterpillars doing the rumba. I laughed but Diane ignored his antics. She was rubbing her eyes.

"Y' know, Uncle Bertie," she said, "It's getting kinda smoky in here."

She flapped a dishtowel a few times and coughed.

"The logs were a bit damp, that's all," Uncle Bertie said, "Give it time. I know a thing or two about making fires. I was a Boy Scout, you know. Got every badge going."

By this time wisps of smoke were seeping out from between the sections of stove-pipe. My eyes began to water. Diane coughed again. Uncle Bertie frowned.

"Hmmm," he said reaching for the poker, "Maybe I'll just stir things up a little."

He slid the heavy lid to the back of the stove but that's all he did, because suddenly there was a tremendous bang. The stove seemed to lift right off the floor and the whole house shuddered. Smoke and smuts and I don't know what all, belched out of the stove and skittered across the ceiling. Another billow of dense smoke engulfed Uncle Bertie and as a final insult, the stove-pipes toppled down showering him with soot. He reeled backwards and fell under the kitchen table. Diane and I staggered around blindly, choking and sputtering.

Dad and Mum burst into the room. Waving their arms in an attempt to clear the air they yelled, "Get out, you two, get out!"

We groped our way to the front door, stumbled to the creek and splashed icy water into our stinging eyes. Dad and Mum appeared dragging Uncle Bertie between them.

"Is he all right?" Diane and I called out anxiously, "Is he hurt?"

Sitting him down on the big stone under the apple tree Mum puffed, "He's had a shock but I don't think he's really hurt. Just give him time to get his breath."

Uncle Bertie was holding his head in his hands and taking big gulps of fresh air. Overhead a couple of starlings flapped their wings and screeched furiously.

"What's the matter with them?" Diane asked.

Dad looked up, thought for a minute and then said, "I bet they built their nest on top of our chimney. Once the fire got going, the smoke couldn't get out so it sort of back-fired. Must have blown their nest to kingdom come, poor things."

Uncle Bertie raised his head. We gasped. His blue eyes sparkled more than ever in his sooty face but his caterpillar eyebrows were singed right down to the roots! His curly eyelashes were nothing but shriveled stumps. Worst of all, the mop of black curls at the front of his head was all twizzled and rust coloured.

"Poor things, my eye!" Uncle Bertie protested, "What about me? I could've been blown to smithereens!"

"Well you weren't," laughed Dad, "But you're not the handsome dog you used to be."

"What d'ya mean?" Uncle Bertie demanded indignantly.

Diane and I pulled him to the creek to look at his reflection in the water. He raised a trembling hand to trace the smudge where his magnificent eyebrows used to be. He ran a shaky finger along his stumpy eyelashes and patted the wiry fringe on his forehead in disbelief. We tried to look sympathetic but we giggled instead.

I don't remember how long it took for Uncle Bertie to recover his good looks but I know that he never came to Stonefield on the 24th of May again. He said he didn't want to miss all the fireworks in the park but we didn't believe him. Would you?

Chapter 2

Teeth, Talk and Tea

We always enjoyed visiting after supper with our next-door neighbors on their big veranda. Mrs. Byrne positioned her rocking chair so she had a clear view all the way to the corner. Mr. Byrne, their daughter Maeve, Mum and Aunt Polly sat on straight-backed chairs facing the Bar X Hotel across the way. Large white letters on the store-front window above their heads advertised the Salada Tea that used to be sold when the Byrne's general store was in operation. Extra chairs were always set out for anyone else who might drop by but Ross and Cheryl and Diane I sat on the floor and dangled our legs over the edge of the verandah.

Léo Lamarche, Maeve's boyfriend, lived in a stone house up the road at the corner. Maeve kept her eyes glued to his front door and as soon as Léo came out, she sprang up and invited us kids to go along with her to meet him half-way. He always greeted her with a loud kiss and then pretended not to know us.

"You must be Marilyn Monroe," he said politely to Cheryl because she had blonde hair, "pleased to meet you."

"What's new with you, Superman?" he asked Ross, "Was that you I saw running up to the swimming hole with your towel, -er, your cape streaming out behind you?"

Diane was next, "Well, if it ain't Veronica Lake," he grinned, ruffling her dark hair.

When it was my turn, he stared hard at me and asked with a perfectly straight face, "Who are you?"

"You know," I replied and right away he came back with, "Of course, how could I forget? You're Miss You Know!"

When Léo took his place on the verandah, he pulled his chair as close to Maeve as he could get and held her hand.

In those days, children were expected to be seen but not heard so while the adults chatted, we kids listened. Sometimes they talked about which crop was ready or where the best raspberries could be found, but their favorite topic by far was the health of their neighbours. A person who was sallow of complexion was labelled 'liverish', while anyone who coughed was declared to be 'bronchial'. They clucked sadly about one family who were known to have 'heart'.

"Don't we all?" I wondered, but I knew better than to ask.

Gall was a common complaint in Stonefield. Mrs. Byrne herself was prone to attacks so she kept a box of pills at the ready in her apron pocket. If anyone present mentioned stomach ache, indigestion or a windy feeling, she pulled out her pills and kindly offered instant relief.

The greatest sympathy of all was reserved for anyone who was 'in bed under the doctor'. The adults always gasped in horror when this was reported, but we kids sniggered into our hands.

The time that Léo reported that his Ma Tante Alphonsine had been in bed under the doctor for the last 3 days, we couldn't hold back. We laughed out loud.

Mum and Aunt Polly were very cross and scolded us severely, but Léo sprang to our defense, "I can see why they're laughing," he said, "Docteur Lafrance is a man who likes his food and Ma Tante is sort of hammered down and rounded off herself. Quite a picture when you come to think of it!"

Once in a while there was a whisper of scandal. As soon as the adults resorted to nods, winks and throat clearings, we kids pricked up our ears. We became very adept at figuring out which baby had arrived suspiciously early or whose husband was spending too much time 'you know where' with 'you'll never guess who' doing 'God knows what.'

Sometimes Léo's parents, M. and Mme. Lamarche joined us on the verandah. We kids were always pleased to see them because we were very interested in their dental arrangements. They actually shared one set of dentures and what's more, their teeth were like our Sunday shoes – kept in a box and only worn on special occasions. Unfortunately the teeth didn't fit either one of them properly.

They slid around and clicked and whistled whenever they spoke. It was most exciting when it was M. Lamarche's turn for the teeth because he shouted to emphasize critical points in his stories. Sooner or later the 'plates' flew right out of his mouth. Ross and Diane made a game out of trying to catch them before they hit the verandah floor. They kept score with the loser having to stump up a dime -- once they got home of course and well out of sight of Mum and Aunt Polly.

Mme. Lamarche, on the other hand, spoke slowly and carefully when it was her turn for the teeth. It was only when she laughed too much that they fell out. In her case, she retrieved the teeth herself because they always landed on her ample bosom.

Often Léo's brothers Eustache and Pierre-Paul turned up with fiddle and guitar to entertain us with jigs and reels. Mrs. Byrne, being a somewhat corpulent lady, step-danced while remaining seated in her rocking chair. Diane and Ross swung each other around until they were too dizzy to stand while Cheryl and I did a few lively dos-si-dos and sashayed up and down the length of the verandah.

To round off the evening the Byrnes invited us to join them for a little lunch before we set off for home. We trooped inside and crowded around their kitchen table. The fiddle was laid carefully on the sideboard, the guitar was placed upright in the corner and the teeth were dropped into a glass of water for safe-keeping. We tucked into tomato sandwiches, slices of chocolate cake and cup after cup of strong black tea. Conversation continued in an untidy mixture of French and English and much head-nodding and waving of hands when words failed us.

At last it was time for bed. We went out to the verandah to count the stars and look for the man in the moon. We said good-night to everyone and drifted home filled with the peace that comes from shared talk and laughter, lively music and simple food. Such wonderful neighbours, such simple pleasures. How lucky we were.

We all pitch in to help bring in the hay. (Circa 1952)

Chapter 3

The Long Hot Summer

The summer of 1947 was terribly hot. Day after day the sun rolled across the sky scorching everything in its path. If the farmers got their hay cut and raked before nine in the morning it was dry enough to load onto the wagons by half-past three in the afternoon. If the housewives got their washing on the line before ten, the clothes were dry as a bone by 1 o'clock. Otherwise there wasn't too much that was good about the intense heat.

The women grumbled because their husbands expected them to light the stove and cook hot meals three times a day and the men complained because their wives served dry cereal for breakfast, cold meat for lunch and jellied salads for supper. They nearly rioted when the children brought ice-cold lemonade and store-bought biscuits to the hayfield instead of the usual scalding hot tea and freshly-baked scones. Babies suffered from heat rash and old people struggled to catch their breath just walking from the kitchen to their chairs on the porch.

The drinking water came out warm from the pump and the milk went sour before you could turn around. Our creek slowed to a trickle and the grass turned as yellow as straw. It was so hot we kids couldn't run around outside. We stayed indoors and tried to play cards but our legs stuck to the chairs and the cards stuck to each other. We read books until the print was nearly worn off the pages and our fingers left sweat marks on the covers. We bickered over nothing and quarreled about everything else.

Even the dog felt the heat. He chased the cows from the barn to the field after the morning milking, barking his fool head off all the way, but at the end of the day he lay panting in the shadiest corner of the yard and didn't even blink when the cows lumbered past for the afternoon milking.

The grown-ups talked endlessly about the heat and how to cope with it. One neighbour advised Mum and Aunt Polly to close all the windows and doors and draw the blinds to keep the heat out of the house. We crept around in the dark for a couple of hours with nothing to do, getting hotter and crosser by the minute before they abandoned that idea. Someone else told us to push our windows up as high as they could go and prop all the doors open to let the air circulate, but the air didn't move and we ended up with a house full of hornets and horse flies to add to our misery.

Another lady was adamant that the best way to keep cool was to drink lots of tea, and the hotter the better. As soon as she was out of earshot, her husband whispered that his home-made spruce beer was much more effective and slipped us a couple of bottles to try. It tasted awful and burned our throats.

Mum and Aunt Polly came to the conclusion that an early lunch and a nap on the linoleum of the living room floor might help us get through the day. They were right. We dozed off soothed by the sweet coolness of the floor and the voice of Aunt Polly telling us long, complicated stories. When we woke up around 4 o'clock it was cool enough to go for a swim and play outside until suppertime. The nights, however, remained a problem. The upstairs bedrooms were stiflingly hot. We tossed and turned until nearly midnight and dozed fitfully until the blazing sun woke us up a few hours later.

One morning after a particularly restless night we stumbled downstairs to find that Mum and Aunt Polly had the picnic basket already packed and our bathing suits and towels neatly folded. Our straw hats teetered on top of the pile.

"Where are we going?" we asked, still rubbing the sleep from our eyes.

"To the By-wash," Mum said, dabbing at the perspiration on her forehead.

"For the whole day," Aunt Polly added, fanning herself with her apron, "because today's going to be a real stinker."

"Hurray, hurray," we yelled.

The By-wash was just about our favourite spot in Stonefield. Part of its attraction was that we were not allowed to go there on our own but mostly we loved it for its sheer beauty. It was located about half-way between our lock, number 5 and lock number 6. To get there we had to walk a considerable distance along the tow-path on the far side of the canal. There were no people living within shouting distance and the surrounding vegetation was so lush that it was easy to pretend we were in a different world altogether.

We could hear the rushing water before we could see it. We kids ran ahead and looked down at the wide staircase that had been carved out of the shale a hundred years before. We watched with fascination as water from the canal overflowed and cascaded onto the first step. It shattered into a million sparkling drops and swirled away in a rush of bubbles and foam. Tall trees bowed to each other from either bank making a lovely green arch above our heads. The sun broke through here and there dappling the water with silver and gold. Mist wafted upwards in gentle billows and cooled our hot faces. Birds flashed in and out of the leaves and frogs croaked from their watery hiding places.

We breathed in the deliciously fresh air and shivered with anticipation. Mum and Aunt Polly led us through the trees to the place where the By-wash emptied into the Ottawa River. We kicked off our shoes and clambered out onto the wet stones, gasping as the cold water eddied around our ankles. We scampered up and down the steps, splashing each other and shrieking with sheer joy. Mum and Aunt Polly settled themselves in a shady nook and watched through half-closed eyes as we turned to building dams and water-falls. For the first time in many weeks we were all comfortable. The fatigue that had dogged our footsteps for so long vanished.

At lunchtime we perched on the grassy bank to eat our sandwiches and drink lemonade. Everything tasted wonderful. Afterwards we climbed higher up the By-wash to explore the shadowy recesses and hunt for polly-wogs.

The day slipped by and we headed for home at sunset refreshed in mind and body. The cool beauty of the By-wash drew us back many times over the years, but that particular day glistens in my mind's eye like a bright star in the evening sky.

A day at the By-wash. (1947)

Chapter 4

The Wedding

The first thing we did when we arrived in Stonefield for the summer was run to the Byrnes' house. Diane and I were always anxious to show them how tall we'd grown over the winter and Mum was anxious to hear about all the doings in Stonefield. I recall that the year I was seven years old, Mrs. Byrne had nothing to say about who died or who had a new baby, but we could see she was bursting with news of some kind or other.

"You'll never guess," she said with a smug grin before Mum had even finished saying hello, "So I'll give you a hint. Somebody not a million miles from here is getting married."

"Maeve," Mum cried, "Léo finally popped the question! That's the best news I've heard in ages!"

Maeve waved her left hand for us to inspect the diamond ring sparkling on her slender finger. Diane and I threw our arms around her waist and hugged her tight.

Maeve helped Mrs. Byrne brew a pot of tea and we all hitched our chairs up to the kitchen table. The three women began to make plans. Diane and I listened impatiently while they talked about taffeta versus lace, leg of mutton or fitted sleeves, and the pros and cons of covered buttons.

I could tell from the frown on Diane's face that she was worrying about the same thing as I was. Both of us were dying to know whether we kids would be getting an invite. Our parents had been to quite a few weddings and we'd been left at home every time.

When we pressed Mum to know why, her answer shocked us and hurt our feelings, "Most people don't want kids running around at a wedding. They get in the way."

But Maeve and Léo weren't most people. They were like a big brother and sister to us and our best friends into the bargain. They went swimming with us, took us for picnics beside the river and thrilled us with exciting rides up and down the mountain roads.

Maeve baked chocolate cakes for late night treats and listened to our troubles. Léo played jokes on us and teased us every chance he got. We giggled with delight when we saw them holding hands and gazing into each other's eyes. We sighed rapturously when they snatched a kiss. Everything about them spelled romance and we wanted to be at their wedding in a bad way.

The talk of wedding finery went on and on with no mention of a guest list. Diane and I got fidgety. Catching my eye, Diane gave me a wink and spoke up when Mum and Mrs. Byrne stopped to have a think about satin pumps with bows or without.

"Can we be excused?" Diane asked politely, "To go out and play?"

"Of course," Mum said absently.

Mum turned to Maeve, "Now, what did you have in mind for your bouquet?"

Outside I squinted in the bright sunlight and asked, "Diane, what d'you think our chances are of getting invited to the wedding?"

"I dunno," she said frowning.

"It wouldn't be rude to ask Maeve or Léo right out would it? After all they like us," I asked.

"I've got a better idea," Diane said decisively, "We'll go and ask Mr. Byrne. He's working on the locks today. He'll give us a straight answer."

We beetled off to the lock-house where Maeve's dad sat peacefully smoking his pipe.

"Any boats coming through?" I asked.

"None so far," he replied with a yawn, "By the way, did youse hear the big news?"

Diane elbowed me so I said hastily, "The wedding, you mean? Yes we did."

With studied casualness, Diane commented, "Prob'ly it's going to be a real wing-ding."

Mr. Byrne nodded and kept puffing.

"Prob'ly be lots of people there too," I said archly.

"Prob'ly," he said nodding his head in agreement.

Diane looked at me and rolled her eyes. This wasn't getting us anywhere.

Taking a deep breath, she planted herself directly in front of him and folding her arms firmly across her chest asked bluntly, "Lookit, we want to know. Are we kids going to be invited to this here wedding or not?"

Mr. Byrne appeared startled by her question. He snatched his pipe out of his mouth and blinked at her a few times.

"Land sakes child, what a question! Of course you're coming to the wedding. I don't think Maeve and Léo would even dream of getting' married if youse weren't there. It wouldn't be any kind of a do at all without youse kids," he said firmly.

When Ross and Cheryl and Aunt Polly arrived on the 1st of August to spend their summer vacation with us, we couldn't wait to tell them about the wedding.

"It's gonna be in Grenville in the big church," Diane informed them, "and the party afterwards will be in the store."

Long ago the Byrnes had operated the local general store. They still lived in the back rooms, but the store itself was a huge empty space. Wide oak counters stood on three sides, and shelves and drawers lined the walls. It was a perfect space for a large gathering.

"Yes, and there's going to be a whole bunch of bridesmaids and grooms," I added, trying to sound knowledgeable. I was crushed when they all laughed at me.

"Don't be silly, Sheila," Ross said, "There's only ever one groom and Léo will be the one at this wedding, that's for sure!"

Kindly Cheryl said, "I'm sure you're right about the bridesmaids though. Maeve's got lots of friends and Léo has umpteen sisters."

"But listen. Best of all, us kids are all invited," Diane yelled.

We shrieked and ran around the yard belting out chorus after chorus of 'Here Comes the Bride'.

From then on, we played wedding every day. Since Ross was the only boy, he had to do double duty. He put his white shirt on backwards when he was the Reverend Father and frontwards when he was the groom. Cheryl and I, as bridesmaids, were gussied up in discarded curtains. We wobbled around in our mums' high heeled shoes clutching limp bouquets of buttercups. Diane paraded back and forth in a wedding gown she rigged up from a tattered lace tablecloth and a threadbare sheet. Carefully we counted down the days on the calendar to August 19.

The wedding day dawned gray and rainy. By ten o'clock the path to the Byrnes' front door was a sea of mud. Dressed in all the rain gear we could muster, we squelched across the yard and knocked on their back door. Mum and Aunt Polly carried in the bridesmaids' bouquets they had put together the day before. Daddy came next balancing trays of food under a large umbrella while Uncle Len followed dragging my old baby carriage loaded down with buckets of ice for the drinks.

When Mrs. Byrne pulled open the kitchen door she was holding a statue of the Virgin Mary high above her head.

"Come in, come in," she cried, "I'm just letting Mary see the rain. Pray that she finds a way to stop it. Maeve's having a fit!"

Maeve was slumped in a chair looking like a crumpled meringue. She was dabbing at her eyes with one of her dad's sturdy red cotton handkerchiefs.

"It's pouring," she wailed, "My wedding's ruined before it's even got started."

"You look beautiful, rain or no rain, Maeve," Mum said soothingly.

"Just like Cinderella," Diane chirped.

"Happy the bride the sun shines on-- oops, sorry," Cheryl stammered going very red in the face.

Maeve wailed, "How am I going to get to the taxi? My shoes'll get soaked and my dress'll be as wet as a dishrag."

She hiccupped and sobbed, "Oh dear, oh dear. What am I going to do?"

Mr. Byrne was pacing from the front door to the back door puffing furiously on his pipe and muttering crossly, "Sunny the whole danged summer and it has to rain today. Can you imagine? All spring we was prayin' for rain to get the garden goin' and not a drop fell. Now look at this, a regular flood when we don't dang well need it."

Mrs. Byrne patted Maeve's shoulder with one hand all the while waving the statue of the blessed Virgin in the general direction of the window.

"Don't cry pet, she'll hear our prayers," she kept repeating.

Maeve sobbed even harder, "If she cares at all, why is it raining today of all days? Answer me that! For two pins I'd call the whole thing off."

Mr. Byrne stopped in his tracks and steepled his fingers as he did when he was thinking.

"Your weddin's goin' ahead if I have to carry you to the church myself!" he announced.

Ross elbowed Diane in the ribs and they grinned. Mr. Byrne was barely five feet tall and on the weedy side. Maeve was a full head taller than her father and plump to bursting.

Daddy and Uncle Len looked up from where they were packing chunks of ice around bottles of beer and soft drinks.

"Tell you what, Maeve," joked Uncle Len, "Bill and I'll load you in this old carriage and wheel you to the church."

Maeve's eyes bugged out. Mum and Aunt Polly shot warning looks at the men.

Maeve shrieked, "I am not being trundled to my wedding in any ramshackle old carriage. I'd rather die."

I began to feel very nervous. It would be just too bad to get this close to my very first wedding only to have the whole thing cancelled.

"I was only joking, Maeve," said Uncle Len, " I promise you that Bill and I will get you out of here and into the taxi safe and sound. Guaranteed!"

"You bet!" Daddy agreed. He sounded very confident but I heard him whisper behind his hand, " Gee whiz Len, how exactly are we going to do that?"

"Roll up your sleeves and follow me," Uncle Len whispered back.

Turning to us, he began to bark out orders like an army sergeant.

"Ross, grab a hold of a chair and put it right near the door. Diane, you skedaddle outside and when Mr. Dansereau gets here tell him to pull his taxi close to the steps.

Cheryl, you and Sheila hold up Maeve's train and veil. Maeve, you hitch up your skirts and hang on. Léo's waiting for his bride."

Maeve gathered her voluminous skirt into her lap. Cheryl and I tucked her train and veil behind her back. Mrs. Byrne whispered a fervent Hail Mary.

Mr. Byrne snatched up an umbrella and held the door open as wide as it would go.

"One, two, three, heave," Uncle Len commanded, "One, two, three, heave!"

Daddy's knees sagged a bit when they hoisted Maeve aloft. We could hear her muffled screams as they staggered through the door. The trip down the steps was a bit dodgy. Mr. Byrne managed to poke both Daddy and Uncle Len in the eye with the umbrella and narrowly escaped falling flat on his face when he missed the last step.

Mr. Dansereau, the taxi-driver, covered his eyes and gasped when they dumped Maeve out of the chair head first into the back seat of the car.

"Mon Dieu," he muttered under his breath, "Pauvre petite mariée."[1]

Red-faced and puffing, Daddy and Uncle Len carried the empty chair back to its usual place at the kitchen table and clapped each other on the back.

"There," Daddy said proudly, "All done and dusted."

Mrs. Byrne put the statue of the blessed Virgin back on top of the piano and went in search of her hat and purse. Mr. Byrne pinned on his boutonnière and trotted out to the waiting taxi.

"C'mon everyone," Diane yelled excitedly, "Get a move on. We're going!"

As our little caravan wound its way up the road, the rain stopped and the sun came out.

Mrs. Byrne rolled down her car window and called back to us, "See? I told you Mother Mary'd help us."

The taxi drew up in front of the church. Mr. Dansereau helped Maeve out of the car while we scampered ahead to take our places inside. The organ wheezed, 'Here Comes the Bride' and six bridesmaids in blue chiffon dresses and huge picture hats swarmed down the aisle ahead of Maeve.

We hummed the familiar tune under our breath as Maeve swept regally past us on her father's arm. Mr. Byrne and Leo's dad were grinning from ear to ear and their wives were weeping tears of joy as Maeve and Léo exchanged vows, rings and kisses. The organ wheezed again and the happy couple came down the aisle. The guests followed them outside and gathered on the steps for a group photograph. Mr. Byrne waved to us kids to move closer to the front.

"Make sure you get these here four kids in the picture," he instructed the photographer, "If it hadn't been for their help Léo and Maeve might not have got married today."

We were still smiling when we piled into the car and made our way back to Stonefield for the reception. Inside the house, the guests lined up to kiss Maeve and congratulate Léo. Relatives showed off new babies, traded family gossip and asked silly questions like, 'Well now, where does the time go?' and 'Why don't we get together more often?'

Daddy soon had the suds flowing for the men and Uncle Len handed round

---

[1] Poor little bride

glasses of elderberry wine to all the ladies. The noise level rose a notch or two.

Mum and Aunt Polly bustled between the kitchen and the store, setting out plates of sandwiches and sweets on the long counters, along with every kind of pickle you could think of.

"Look at all that food," Ross marveled, "What should we try first?"

Dodging elbows and handbags we darted around to inspect the platters.

I was trying to decide between a ham or egg salad sandwich when Diane grabbed me and said excitedly, "Sheila, come over here and see what we found!"

She clutched my arm and dragged me around and through the blue suits and flowered dresses to the far side of the room where Ross and Cheryl were standing shoulder to shoulder shielding something from view.

Diane shoved me between them and spoke out of the corner of her mouth, "Turn around, casual like and see what's there."

I was used to her take-charge ways and did as I was told. She didn't often steer me wrong, but all I saw was an oblong dish holding carrot sticks and pieces of celery.

"What's the big deal?" I complained, "It's only boring old vegetables."

Diane jabbed a finger towards the dish and said impatiently, "Check it again, dopey.

That there's not just celery. It's stuffed celery!"

I leaned closer and sure enough, each little chunk of celery was filled with a strip of orange cheese.

"Isn't that something?" Cheryl marveled, "Better grab it now before everyone sees it."

By now the guests were enthusiastically filling their plates and the conversation became more and more animated as Uncle Len and Daddy topped up their glasses.

We kids went into action. We scuttled the length of the counters, sneakily sliding all the stuffed celery off the dishes and onto our plates. We munched greedily while the fiddles were tuned. We were still chewing when Léo and Maeve whirled around the floor in their first dance.

"What's next?" asked Ross, when there was no more celery to be had.

"Dessert!" I suggested, but before we could make a move, Léo's dad, M. Lamarche bawled, "Take your partners for the Paul Jones. Youse kids too."

"You mean, we can join in?" Ross asked doubtfully, "We can really dance with everyone?"

"B'en oui," he roared, "It wouldn't be no kind of a dance without youse kids."

I was thrilled to bits. A wedding, stuffed celery and now dancing! My feet barely touched the floor as M. Tremblay, the laundryman, waltzed me around the room.

Diane spun by with Mr. Swinton, the local baker and I spied Ross manfully doing his best to maneuver a very substantial woman across the dance floor.

Jigs and reels followed one after the other and the adults patiently guided us through the unfamiliar steps. It was more fun that we could ever have imagined.

"What're youse talkin' about?" said one of our neighbours when we pleaded fatigue, "No one gets tired dancin' at a weddin'. Youse jist keep goin'."

So we whooped and hollered with the best of them and even took our turns in the center of the floor to step dance. Sweat poured down the faces of the fiddlers and still the guests called for more until Mrs. Byrne silenced the musicians with a wave of her hand and announced, "Time to cut the cake!"

Three tiers high and swathed in glistening white icing, the cake looked like something out of a story book. To my delight there was a miniature bride and groom right on the top and the daisies we kids had picked encircled the base.

Everyone gathered around Léo and Maeve. The photographer snapped a picture and a cheer went up as the silver knife slid through the cake.

"Are we going to keep dancing?" I asked Cheryl, "I think I'm getting the hang of the Chicken Reel."

"Don't you know anything?" she sighed, "Once the cake has been cut that means the dancing is over. Léo and Maeve will leave pretty soon for their honeymoon."

Slices of wedding cake were passed around. Cups of tea and coffee were served to wash it down and the guests spilled out on to the verandah to wave good-bye to the happy couple.

Ross and Cheryl and Diane and I followed them right to the car tossing handfuls of confetti all the way.

Maeve leaned down to give us a kiss good-bye and said, "Léo and I want to say a special thank-you to youse kids. You helped save the day."

We were so proud and happy that for once we were struck dumb. Handkerchiefs fluttered.

Mrs. Byrne and Mme. Lamarche wept in each other's arms. Léo and Maeve's car turned the corner and disappeared up the road. Mr. Byrne came to stand beside us.

"Well now, did youse have a good time?" he asked.

Diane nodded, "I never tasted such wonderful wedding cake in my entire life."

"I liked the stuffed celery best of all," I answered remembering the crunch of the celery and the delicious smoothness of the cheese.

Cheryl sighed and said, "Maeve's dress was gorgeous. I want one just like it for my wedding when I grow up."

"I found out that I was a darn good dancer today," Ross bragged.

Mr. Byrne took a long satisfying pull on his pipe.

"It was a great weddin' if I say so myself," he said with a grin, "But it wouldn't have been any kind of a do without youse kids, that's for galldarned sure."

I can't speak for Ross or Cheryl or Diane, but Maeve and Léo's wedding was one of the most memorable days of my life. I have never felt so welcome anywhere as I did that day.

Cheryl and Sheila, the bridesmaids. (1950)

The By-wash
Hand-carved, hidden
Tumbling, gurgling, sparkling
Waterfalls, pools, Eden, Shangri-La
Shining, singing, shouting
Beautiful, unspoiled
Perfection

Chapter 5

Race for the Ice

Mum firmly believed that anything could be cured by a month in the country. "For one thing, the air's so much fresher," she declared, "And for another, there are lots of things to do to take your mind off your troubles."

So when our teenaged cousin Heather suffered a disappointment in love, Mum invited her to spend the month of July with us in Stonefield. At first Heather was very subdued and seldom spoke. She tended to sleep late in the morning and go to bed early at night. When we sat on the porch in the evening to watch the sunset, her mouth drooped and her eyes filled with tears. My sister Diane and I looked for ways to distract her and get her out of the house. We took turns brushing her long hair, cajoled her into teaching us how to jitter-bug and coaxed her to help us with our chores.

Slowly she began to perk up. I must say she was a good sport. She pumped water, picked berries, cleaned oil lamps and chased the occasional bat out of the house without screaming. In no time she was faster than us at stacking fire-wood, neater than us at making beds and a lot less squeamish about emptying mouse traps. But the thing that really put the roses back in her cheeks was a trip to the ice-house.

"We need a fresh block of ice," Mum announced one morning, "Better get yourselves over to Charlie's pretty quick or the milk will be sour by lunchtime."

Diane bumped our old baby carriage out the back door while I grabbed two thick quilts.

"C'mon Heather," we shouted, "You're in for a treat! We'll count the trip there as a practice run 'cause the one that'll really count is the one when we come back with the ice."

I hopped into the carriage and held on to the sides for dear life. Diane grabbed the handle with both hands and told Heather to do the same.

"What we're aiming for, Heather, is to beat our record time of six minutes and 32 seconds, so we have to run like mad. Whatever you do, don't let the carriage tip over. We'll lose a lot of time if we have to stop and pick Sheila up."

Heather looked a little startled but Diane just grinned.

She checked her watch and bellowed, "Ready, steady, go!"

Off we went, sending gravel flying in all directions. The carriage rocked crazily as we careened around the corner, shot past the general store and the hotel and whizzed past the horse barn. Another perilous turn on two wheels and then we hit the smoothest part of the road. We were sailing. Charlie's icehouse was not too far away now. Panting heavily, Diane and Heather gave one last burst of speed and we arrived in a cloud of dust at Charlie's gate, pleased as the dickens and more importantly, right side up.

Diane looked at her watch and said, "What do you know? We beat our record by 14 seconds. Thanks a lot, Heather."

Heather's face was beet-red and she was gasping for breath. She looked slightly dazed by the whole experience. Charlie ambled out to greet us, quite unperturbed by our hectic arrival. He was dressed as usual in ragged brown trousers and the army jacket he had worn every day since he fought in the First World War as a young man. He paused to straighten his service medal and expertly aimed a stream of tobacco-laden saliva into the long grass before speaking.

"How are youse? And who's this pretty little lady youse have with youse today?" he asked politely.

Proudly Diane and I introduced Heather explaining that she was from Montreal and had come to stay with us for a while.

"We're showing her what living in the country is like," Diane told him.

Charlie gave a little bow and said, "Pleased to meet ya, I'm sure. My name's Charlie and I keep the ice-house for all the folks in Stonefield. I got two fine horses," he drawled, "And in the winter I use this here sleigh to draw the ice from the river."

Since Charlie didn't hold with putting anything away, the sleigh really was right there in front of us. In fact, it was something of an obstacle as he'd left it smack dab in front of the ice-house door.

"Wait 'til you see inside, Heather," we said, "You'll love it."

Sauntering on ahead, Charlie reminded us to shut the door to keep out the heat. It was like a different world once the door closed. It was so dark that we had to stand still for a minute or two to get our bearings. It smelled as fresh as a winter day in a pine forest. A thick layer of sawdust formed a soft carpet under our feet. Shivering in the cold we watched as Charlie leisurely perused his stock. He maneuvered his chaw of tobacco from one cheek to the other. Finally he tapped one block.

"This one'll be about right for your Ma's ice-box, I reckon," he said thoughtfully.

"Now where'd I leave my gloves?" he said to no one in particular.

"Excuse me, Charlie, but would these be what you're looking for?" Heather asked. She was holding up a disreputable pair of woolen gloves. The fingers were hacked off about half-way up and the cuffs were unraveling.

Smiling with delight Charlie reached for them, "Now then, that's grand. You got sharp eyes for a city girl."

He pulled on his gloves and carefully brushed the sawdust off our block of ice. Our teeth were beginning to chatter but Charlie couldn't be rushed.

He examined the ice, muttering to himself, "A very nice piece, if I do say so myself. Clear as a bell and no cracks. Look at that. A work of art that is. Marvellous, innit?"

"T-t-terrific," we stuttered, "C-c- can we go outside now, Charlie? We're awfully c-c-cold."

"Are youse now?" Charlie asked sounding surprised, "Go ahead. I'll be ready in two ticks. Now where do you suppose my calipers are?"

He peered around helplessly in the dim light. Knowing that this might happen, Diane had already found them.

She shoved them into Charlie's hand and said, "We'll open the door for you and get the carriage ready."

We scampered around the sleigh in double quick time. I spread one quilt in the bottom of the carriage and held the other one at the ready. Eventually Charlie staggered out of the ice-house, inched his way around the sleigh and dropped the glistening block of ice into the carriage. With lightning speed I wrapped the second quilt around it and sat on top to keep it steady on the ride home. Heather dropped the money into Charlie's woolly paw and helped

Diane drag the carriage out of the yard.

Once they cleared the grassy entrance Diane checked her watch and yelled, "Go!"

They took off as fast as their legs could carry them. Heads down and legs pumping they covered the distance from Charlie's place to the horse barn in no time flat.

"Turn left," I screamed, "Turn, turn."

The wheels skidded on the gravel and I leaned to one side to help them make the curve. Now we were on the straightaway. Diane and Heather were sprinting in perfect rhythm.

"Go, go," I screeched, "I'm freezing and the ice is starting to melt."

We flew past the general store leaving a trail of drops behind us.

"Turn left, hard left," I yelled.

Red-faced and perspiring, Diane and Heather executed the sharp corner on two wheels. Diane and I had often come to grief right there, with me and the carriage upside down and the ice slithering around in the dirt. But not today. Heather's strong arms made all the difference.

"Hurray," I shouted, "we're almost home."

As soon as we reached our front gate, I leaped out and helped pull the carriage across the grass to the back door. Mum was waiting with the ice tongs and in a flash she peeled off the quilt and dragged the heavy block into the house. Straining and sweating, we all helped to heave it up into the ice-box.

Diane looked at her watch and crowed, "Faster than ever, 5 minutes and 27 seconds! You were great Heather. Bet you never had that much fun in the city, did you?"

"Never," Heather laughed. Her face was flushed and her eyes were shining.

That evening when we finished our supper we went out to sit on the porch. As the sun slipped behind the trees, we gave Mum a blow-by-blow account of our record-breaking trip to Charlie's ice-house and back.

"Heather was terrific," I exclaimed, "You should have seen her go. She can run like a deer."

"That was our fastest time yet. You were a big help on the corners, Heather. We never turned over once!" Diane said.

"It was fabulous," Heather sighed, "I haven't run that fast since I don't know when."

"I hope the girls didn't tire you out," Mum said.

Heather's eyes danced with excitement and she laughed, "I'm not a bit tired, Auntie Dorothy. I feel great. In fact I can't wait to do it again."

Mum smiled at Heather and sighed happily, "Like I've always said, a month in the country can cure anything."

Chapter 6

Fire in the Outhouse

July was just about over. Heather's broken heart was mended thanks to fresh air, exercise and her enthusiastic response to country life in general. She cheerfully took over the chores that made Diane and I balk. While we were still looking for the pails through half-closed eyes, Heather was already on her way back from the canal with both pails filled to overflowing. And she never accidentally scooped up minnows or bugs either. We were impressed.

Stacking kindling for the stove actually seemed to be fun for her. She took pride in making a pile that was symmetrical while we were satisfied with a teetering lumpy heap. Before she came to Stonefield, Heather hadn't so much as watered a pot plant. After a month with us she was an enthusiastic gardener. We couldn't understand it because even a simple job like thinning the carrots brought out the worst in Diane and me.

"It's too hot to bend over all morning in the garden," we whined, "The blood rushes to our heads and makes us dizzy."

Heather just laughed and said, "C'mon, it'll be fun. Besides blood rushing to your brain makes you smarter."

Our chores inside and outside the house increased dramatically during the last three days of July. That was because Aunt Polly, Ross and Cheryl were arriving on the first of August to stay for the rest of the summer. Mum went into a positive tailspin of activity.

"Girls, today the downstairs floors and the upstairs windows have to be washed," she announced ticking off the jobs on her fingers, "and tomorrow the spare room mattresses have to be turned and all the bureau drawers lined with fresh paper and cedar boughs." The only thing that appealed to Diane and me was cutting the cedar boughs from the hedge.

"We'll look after the cedar boughs," we offered generously, "Tomorrow."

Heather disappeared with the mop and bucket. Diane and I thought we were home free but Mum drew us up short.

"You two slippery characters get yourselves out to the shed and mix up a pail of white-wash. Sweep the outhouse clean of spiders and slap on two coats. Then look through the magazines and find some nice pictures to put up on the walls."

Mum took great pride in having the brightest, cleanest outhouse in Stonefield. Ours was a two-holer and it was graced with matching toilet seats that Dad painted every year with a coat of the best white enamel. The door was left open between visits to ensure a steady flow of fresh air, and a large pail of ashes stood in the corner at all times with a small shovel hanging nearby. These arrangements were almost as effective as a flush.

"Get busy and no slacking," Mum warned us, "I'll telephone Mr. Dansereau and ask him to drive us to the train to meet Aunt Polly and the kids."

While Heather swabbed floors and polished windows, Diane and I buckled down and soon had the outhouse in pristine condition. We were excited at the prospect of having Ross and Cheryl to play with for the coming month.

"Hey," Diane said to me, eyes sparkling, "What d'ya think Aunt Polly will bring us?"

I stopped painting to think about this important question, "Gee, I dunno," I said, "last year she brought those neat Indian head dresses. The year before that she brought us, um, um…"

"Plaid bathing suits," cried Diane, "Remember? She bought them in the States and nobody else in Canada had anything like them."

The outhouse passed inspection and of course Heather's work was perfectly done. The night before the big day was cold and rainy.

"I think I'll light the fire before we go to bed," Mum decided, "I don't want the house to be damp when Aunt Polly and the kids arrive tomorrow. Get some kindling and a couple of logs, would you, girls? That should get us through the night quite nicely, and they said on the radio that tomorrow will be sunny and dry."

That night our little bedroom under the eaves was snug and warm. The rain drummed on the roof while Diane and I whispered about what might be in Aunt Polly's big steamer trunk with the shiny brass corners.

At breakfast the next morning we talked nineteen to the dozen to Heather about the great times we would have in the coming weeks.

"Ross and Cheryl are really fun to play with. Sometimes we put on shows, singing and dancing kind of thing. Other times we play Cowboys and Indians and when no one's around we go jump in the hay mow in the barn next door.

"Wait'll you meet Aunt Polly," we rattled on, "She can do cartwheels right across the lawn and she makes fudge and shortbread cookies and doesn't mind how much jam we put on our toast. She wears red nail polish all the time and four-inch high heels when we go to town. And," we paused for effect, "She always brings us terrific presents!"

Mum stood up and began to clear the table.

"Mr. Dansereau will be here in half an hour girls. Brush your teeth and wash your faces," she reminded us.

"I'll stay home and tidy up," Heather offered helpfully, "You go and get ready while I start the dishes, Auntie Dorothy."

She poured hot water from the kettle into the dishpan, lathered the soap with the dish mop and began to wash the dishes, whistling cheerfully.

Mr. Dansereau's taxi eased to a careful stop in front of our gate. The visor of his cap gleamed in the sun when he stepped out of the car. His trousers were perfectly pressed and his grey gloves impeccably clean. He held the door open, gently holding Mum by the elbow as she climbed in and sat down.

Holding on to the thick braided velvet cord that hung across the back of the front seats, Diane and I bounced up and down excitedly. We loved riding in the taxi. We loved going to the station and we loved the noise and the clouds of steam when the train pulled into the station. As soon as we heard the shriek of the whistle and the thunder of the huge engine we jumped out of the car.

"They're here, they're here," we screamed, dancing from one foot to the other as the train ground to a halt in front of us.

The trainman placed the little step stool on the platform, Ross jumped down, closely followed by Cheryl. Then Aunt Polly's familiar navy blue and white pumps with the high heels appeared on the step. A huge picture hat shaded her face and she waved a white-gloved hand in our direction.

Mr. Dansereau dealt efficiently with the hand luggage and hoisted the glistening steamer trunk to his shoulder and tied it securely to the roof rack.

The ride back down the Montée resembled a magpie's convention. Ross and Cheryl quizzed Diane and me about what we'd been up to so far. Mum and Aunt Polly bubbled over with plans for the coming weeks. The imperturbable Mr. Dansereau drove us home, made sure we all climbed out in an orderly fashion and deposited the luggage in the hall.

"Pump handle all round[2]," we cried as we introduced Heather to Aunt Polly, Ross and Cheryl.

Heather smiled and shook hands politely with them.

"The kettle's on the boil so I'll go and make the tea," she said and darted back to the kitchen.

Aunt Polly was one of those rare adults who had not forgotten what it was like to be a child. Tossing her hat on to the living room couch, she got right to the point.

Giving us a mischievous wink, she called to Heather, "Keep the water hot for a few more minutes, Heather. I'd better get this trunk open before certain little girls explode."

She turned the key and raised the lid. Right on top we could see a stack of red firemen's hats. She handed them out to Diane and me and Ross and Cheryl.

"There you go. You should have some fun with these," she laughed.

"Gee whiz, what a great present," Diane said while I gave her a big hug.

Heather came to the door to watch the goings on.

"I brought something different for you, Heather. I thought you'd probably be too grown up for a fireman's hat," Aunt Polly said and she handed Heather a dainty pink sun hat with white pompoms all around the edge. Heather was thrilled.

Mum said, "Now you kids go outside. I know you're dying to play with those hats. Have fun!"

The four of us dashed outside leaving the screen door swinging crazily

---

[2] Shake hands with everyone

on its hinges. We tore all over the yard, under the swing, through the raspberry canes, around the patch of Golden Glow and over the huge boulder near the woodshed. We suddenly realized that Heather wasn't with us.

"Come out, Heather," Diane called through the kitchen window, "You can play too, you know."

"Let's pretend the house is burning down," Cheryl yelled.

"You three girls can be the firemen and I'll be the chief, "Ross volunteered, "and you can be the engine driver, Heather."

Obligingly Heather began to wail like a siren. She took off at top speed and screeched to a halt by the back door.

"Quick, men, there's not much time. This whole house will be a pile of rubble if you don't hurry," she yelled.

Ross took over shouting orders at us as we scuttled around," Okay men, aim the hose at the roof, break down the door, stamp out those flames. Get a move on."

We soon tired of that situation so we pretended to rescue a cat from the elm tree. Having dealt with that crisis we turned to saving children from a burning school, followed by a hair-raising game of leading terrified horses from a smoke-filled barn. We were thrilled to discover that Heather could whinny and squeal like a real horse.

Meanwhile in the dining room, Mum and Aunt Polly were completely engrossed in conversation. They had not seen each other for several weeks and had a lot of catching up to do. Mum named the neighbors she had already visited and Aunt Polly made a list of everyone she wanted to call on too. They counted the empty jam jars in the pantry and made plans for several trips to the berry patch. I don't think they even heard our blood-curdling screams or Ross bellowing orders at the top of his lungs. They paid no attention when we went quiet either. Worn out, we flopped on the grass to rest for a while.

It was Cheryl who sat up first and said slowly, "Hey look, there's smoke coming out of the outhouse."

"Very funny," I said not bothering to raise my head.

"I'm not joking. Look!" she insisted.

"You're not going to get me this time," I answered, "Last year you always played tricks on me but I'm eight now and it won't work any more."

Heather chuckled and said, "I'm new to the country but even I know that smoke doesn't come out of an outhouse."

Cheryl stood up indignantly and pointing at the outhouse told us to look for ourselves. We ignored her.

"Shut up, Cheryl," said Ross, "I'm trying to think up another game."

Taking a deep breath, Cheryl bawled, "Fire! Fire! Fire in the outhouse!"

Shocked, we leapt to our feet. Sure enough, there was smoke curling out of the knotholes and chinks in the walls of the outhouse.

All five of us began charging around shouting, "Fire! Fire! Fire in the outhouse!"

Our mothers didn't appear. Clutching our red helmets we raced into the house screaming the news, "Fire! Fire! Fire in the outhouse!"

Mum and Aunt Polly were very annoyed by our noisy intrusion and shooed us out the back door.

"It's rude to shout in the house. Come in when you can speak quietly."

Frantically we ran around to the front door and burst into the house again.

"Fire! Fire! Fire in the outhouse," we screamed.

This time Mum got really cross. Hands on hips, she spoke firmly, "We've already told you to stay outside if you're going to shout your heads off. We have things to do. Play your nice fireman game and don't bother us for ten minutes at least."

By this time the smoke was billowing out of the outhouse and little yellow flames were licking at the door-frame. Ross and Cheryl and Diane and I had no idea what to do.

Stupidly we hopped around and yelled at each other, "Fire! Fire! Fire in the outhouse!"

Thank goodness for Heather. She darted into the woodshed and came back lugging the two pails of water she had taken from the canal that morning. She disappeared into the outhouse and doused the fire.

When she staggered out, she was all smudged and dirty. We ran to meet her and sat her down on a nearby tree stump.

"You were wonderful, Heather. You saved our lives," cried Diane.

"Well, the outhouse anyway," Ross said.

To our surprise Heather began to weep uncontrollably.

"The fire was my fault," she sobbed, "and it could have spread to the barn on the other side of the fence and burned down half of Stonefield."

We were baffled. Diane was the first to speak.

"What do you mean?" she asked, "How can it be your fault? You were playing with us the whole time and we never went near the outhouse."

"That's right," we chorused, "How could it be your fault? Don't be silly."

We were so busy comforting Heather that we didn't notice that Mum and Aunt Polly had finally appeared on the scene.

"What's that awful smell?" asked Mum, "Is Flossie cooking outside again?"

Our eccentric neighbour sometimes boiled up some pretty smelly brews on the old wood stove in her yard.

"Not this time, Mum," I said but before I could explain further, Aunt Polly gasped and pointed at the blackened outhouse.

This set Heather off again good and proper. She cried even harder. Hiccoughing and choking she stammered, "Auntie Dorothy, after you l-l-left for the st-st-station I decided to riddle the ashes out of the st-st-stove. I've seen you do it and I was just tr-tr-trying to be helpful. I didn't mean to cause tr-tr-trouble."

"Now, now dear," Mum said, "Never mind about the outhouse. Take a deep breath and tell me exactly what happened."

"Well," Heather said shakily, "like I said, I scraped all the ashes together just the way I've seen you do, but I couldn't find the pail to put them in so I-I-I".

Her voice rose an octave or two and she finished her sentence in a breathless squeal, "I put the ashes in the cardboard box I found in the pantry."

Aunt Polly handed Heather her hankie and we waited while Heather mopped her face. She took a ragged breath and went on, "Then I carried the box to the outhouse and put it on the fl-fl-floor."

Mum spoke sympathetically, "Oh dear, there must have been some embers left among the ashes. You weren't to know, but that's why I always put them in a metal pail."

Heather burst into tears all over again.

"That means I caused the fire, doesn't it? Oh, Auntie Dorothy, are you going to send me h-h-home?" she wailed, " 'cause I didn't mean to do it. I really didn't."

Mum looked shocked, "Send you home? Of course I won't send you home. You just made a mistake. It could happen to anybody. You're staying right here with us. We've got a whole month of fun in front of us, haven't we?"

Whooping and hollering we kids began to race around the yard. Aunt Polly did a few cartwheels and Mum gave Heather a comforting hug. After inspecting the outhouse Mum declared that it was still usable.

"A fresh coat of whitewash and a couple of new boards in the floor and it'll be good as new," she announced.

Ross couldn't resist nailing his fireman's helmet to the outhouse door. He said it was to remind himself of the most exciting start he'd ever had to his summer holidays.

Cows
shy brown-eyed beauties
lowing at the gate
heavy with milk
Waiting

Stone Fence
Ancient, weather-beaten
Separating, defining, protecting
Home to the chipmunks
As old as the hills
Guardian

Chapter 7

Bulgy Higgins

Bulgy Higgins' false teeth were blindingly white and straight as tombstones but other than that they were a disappointment.

"Took me the best part of the winter to scratch up enough dough for these here choppers and they're no danged good at all," he complained, "I can't even bite the skin on a rice puddin' without them pinchin' like the divil himself."

We tried to encourage him, "Give them a chance, Bulgy. You'll get used to them."

It turned out we were right.

"They're grand for keeping my pipe steady," he told us gleefully one day and showed us how he could clamp it between his teeth so tight it didn't wobble or droop one bit.

Diane and I and Ross and Cheryl knew Bulgy well because he and Mr. Byrne were working at Lock 5 in front of our house. They called us their assistants and we always did whatever they asked, except for that shameful afternoon when Bulgy desperately needed our help and we didn't lift a finger.

Here's what happened.

"Howdy strangers, how are youse?" Mr. Byrne and Bulgy greeted us from their usual spot on the bench under the trees.

"Fine, but did we miss any boats this morning?" asked Diane, "We had to go berry picking right after breakfast and we just got back."

"Not a one. Good thing too seeing as how youse weren't around," remarked Bulgy, " 'cause we'd never have managed."

His teeth clicked and slid forward and he adjusted them with his thumb before asking, "Did youse get many berries?"

"Tons of them," I sighed, "And it was so hot we nearly died of heat stroke."

"Why don't youse hang around for a while," suggested Mr. Byrne, "There'll prob'ly be a boat or two comin' through before long."

Ross pulled a toy car out of his pocket and he and Diane began to make roads in the gravel around the bench. Cheryl and I flopped on the grass to look for four-leaf clovers.

"If youse'll excuse me, I'll just have 40 winks," yawned Mr. Byrne.

He tipped his cap over his eyes and was soon snoring gently. Bulgy pulled out his pipe and puffed out a halo of smoke.

After a while he announced, "I'm feeling a bit peckish. Time for my snack."

He produced a large orange.

"I'd much rather have a couple of scones with a dab of jam," he told us, "But the missus says I've got to reduce the size of my shadow, so this is it."

Bulgy peeled his orange and stacked the skin on the bench beside him. Then he removed his teeth and placed them carefully on top of the peelings.

He managed to mash the fruit with his gums until it was soft enough to swallow. Bulgy was about to tackle the last piece when the telephone shrilled from the lock-house.

"The phone, the phone," Diane shrieked, "Wake up, Mr. Byrne, wake up!"

Mr. Byrne scurried off to take the call. A minute later he burst out of the lock house to announce that three yachts were on their way from Lock 4. We began shouting to each other to get to work. Diane and Ross took their places next to the big iron gears and stood ready to crank open the gates. Cheryl and I ran to the swing bridge and summoning all our strength, lifted the heavy handle and put it in place.

"C'mon Bulgy," Ross called impatiently, "We're ready and waiting over here."

"We're all set up here," Cheryl yelled.

"Keep your hair on," he yelled back, "I'll be there in a jiffy."

That's when poor Bulgy made a terrible mistake. He scooped up the orange peels, ran to the edge of the canal and tossed them into the water. Suddenly he clapped his hand to his forehead and screamed, "My teeth, my teeth!"

We looked down into the lock and watched open-mouthed as Bulgy's teeth floated on top of the orange peels for a minute or two before sinking slowly out of sight in the blue-black water.

Frantically Bulgy pleaded with us, "One of youth dive in and feth 'em, for pity'th thake. Quick! You know I can't thwim."

We leaned over for a closer look, but none of us took the plunge.

"Good-bye toothy-pegs," Cheryl sang out.

Naughtily I waved and blew kisses, "It's been nice knowin'ya."

"Ta-ta teeth," called Ross, wrapping his lips around his teeth in a deadly imitation of poor toothless Bulgy.

"If I catch a fish wearing your pearly whites I'll let you know, Bulgy," Diane yelled cheekily.

Mr. Byrne took off his cap and scratched his head, "Gee whiz Bulgy, I'd love to help you but I can't swim a stroke myself."

His voice was full of sympathy for Bulgy but we kids were laughing too hard to offer one word of consolation.

It took Bulgy a whole year this time to save up for a new set of teeth. When the poor guy finally got them they looked great but believe it or not, they ended up in the drink too, but that's a story for another day.

Water
Shimmering like silk
slips down the By-wash
a thousand silver threads
catch on sharp stones
spin in whirlpools
and weave their way
into the rough waves of the river
Invisible

Snake
Striped, bright-eyed
Slithering, winding, wriggling
Making us shiver
As silent as time
A threat

Chapter 8

Missing Shingles

In the summer of 1951 our roof was leaking so badly that we used our biggest soup pot to catch the drips at the top of the stairs, the tin washtub to handle the deluge in the hall and our spare chamber pot for the overflow in the back bedroom.

After a particularly rainy spell Dad said, "It's too far gone to patch. I'll have to re-shingle the whole thing and the sooner the better."

"You're right," agreed Mum, "It doesn't do to neglect a roof."

"What colour would you like, dear?" asked Dad.

"Red, and the brighter the better," she replied

A few days later Diane and I woke to hear Dad hard at work on the roof. We bolted our breakfast, shot outside and clambered up onto the huge boulder behind our house to get a little closer to the action.

"Hey Dad," we called up to him, "Can we help?"

"Well, let me see," he answered, "Maybe you could just hold a steady course right where you are and keep me company."

"I could climb up the ladder and hand you things," Diane offered.

"I'd be happier if you just stayed put," said Dad hastily.

While Dad worked Diane and I chattered away. Dad nodded his head from time to time or puffed out an absent-minded, "You don't say," while hammering down row after row of new red shingles. Eventually our conversation petered out and we sat in silence for a few minutes.

Across the field next to our place I noticed our neighbours pottering about in the maze that passed for their garden.

"Look Diane," I said, "There's Flossie and Jack. Let's pretend we're announcers on the radio and we'll report what they're doing."

"Good idea. That could be fun," Diane said and immediately went into action.

"This is radio station RSVP 200 on your dial, bringing you an up-to-date report on a late breaking news story."

Her voice rose with excitement, "Jack's checking his raspberry canes. Stay tuned folks. Anything could happen!"

I broke in, "My goodness! You may find this hard to believe, listeners at home, but Flossie is actually pulling some rhubarb."

Flossie and Jack were famous for their devotion to each other and their neglect of almost everything else.

If the day was hot Flossie said to her husband, "Jack dear, I don't think you should work in the fields today. You might take heat stroke, and then where would we be?"

If the day was wet she said, "Jack my love, I don't think you should go out today. You might take a chill and then where would we be?"

Jack appreciated his wife's advice and was equally concerned for her welfare. When their kitchen garden was choked with weeds he said, "Flossie my sweet, don't lift that hoe. You might do yourself a mischief and then where would we be?"

True to form Jack and Flossie stopped their activities and stood as still as statues.

Diane hesitated and then cleverly improvised, "Things are at a standstill so we'll bring you a message from our sponsor. Don't touch that dial, we'll be right back."

I sang one chorus of a popular soap jingle, "Duz does everything!" and Diane finished off with, "You'll wonder where the yellow went, when you brush your teeth with Pepsodent."

Flossie and Jack drifted across their yard.

"Welcome back, audience at home," Diane said warmly, "We're happy to tell you that our neighbours are back in action. They appear to be heading for their bench. They're almost there. They've made it ladies and gentlemen.

They're sitting down even as I speak. Jack's fanning his face with his hat."

That bench was all Flossie and Jack had in the way of garden furniture and it was actually just a rough board resting on a couple of tree stumps.

"Hang on," Diane continued, "There's a new development. Blackie's coming out of his doghouse. Don't touch that dial, folks. Dogs can be unpredictable. He's ambling over to join Flossie and Jack. He's there. Flossie's patting him and Jack's scratching his ears."

She added hastily, "The dog's I mean, not his own. I think Blackie's going to lie down. He is! He's turning around. Stay with us, listeners. One, two, three turns," she counted, "and he's down! He's going to have a snooze!"

By this time, Dad was hopelessly distracted so he edged closer to watch Jack and Flossie for himself. His gaze roamed over their wild garden before coming to rest on the roof of their house.

"Holy smoke," he gasped, "Their roof is in worse shape than ours. It must leak like a sieve."

That night we heard Dad telling Mum about Jack's gap-toothed roof, "We're going to have shingles left over," said Dad, "What do you say I offer them to Flossie and Jack?"

"That's a good idea," she said, "They'll probably be thrilled."

Diane and I tagged along a week later when Dad delivered a wheelbarrow full of shingles. Flossie and Jack were on their bench enjoying the sunshine. Blackie was dozing peacefully at their feet and although he didn't raise his head he welcomed us with a few thumps of his tail.

"Well now," drawled Jack with a wink, "Sit down and take a load off your mind."

The bench sagged alarmingly when Diane and I sat down so Dad stayed standing.

"Maybe you've noticed me shingling my roof," he began.

Jack nodded, "Yup, I seen you hauling them heavy bundles up there. Me and Flossie was a mite worried. You could've had a rapture[3] and then where would you be?"

Flossie looked concerned, "All them hours in the hot sun. However did you manage?"

Diane and I were pleased when Dad said we'd kept him entertained.

He continued, "I couldn't help noticing that you're missing a few shingles."

[3] rupture

Flossie and Jack looked up at their roof in astonishment.

"You don't say! You know, you're prob'ly right. It does get a mite damp inside when it rains," Jack said.

"Well then, could you use these shingles?" asked Dad, "I bought more than I needed and it'd be a shame for them to go to waste."

Flossie smiled sweetly, "That's real neighbourly of you. Thank-you."

Dad hoisted a bundle onto his shoulder and asked, "Where should we put them, Jack?"

The question seemed to bewilder Jack, "Geez, I dunno," he said rubbing his bristly chin.

Flossie looked around and said, "We should put them where they'll be handy. Right there under the apple tree will do."

Dad unloaded the wheelbarrow and we headed home.

Weeks drifted by and the shingles languished where Dad had left them. He fumed about idle hands, sloth and ingratitude.

Mum tried to soothe his rising temper, "Now, now. You know Jack takes a while to get around to things. He'll probably do a wonderful job once he puts his mind to it."

Dad just snorted.

Things boiled over one morning in late August just as Diane and I came down to breakfast. Dad was sitting at the table with a cup of coffee, idly looking out the window towards Flossie and Jack's place. Suddenly he leapt up with such force that his chair crashed backwards onto the floor. His eyes bugged out and his mouth sagged open.

"Glory be to Peter!" he roared pointing across the field at Jack and Flossie's place, "Can you believe it? If that doesn't beat all! Look! Look!"

We looked and burst out laughing. No wonder Dad was so mad. Jack hadn't touched his own roof but Blackie's doghouse was completely covered with perfectly straight rows of bright red shingles!

Chapter 9

The Organ Pipes

In the 1950's, everyone in Stonefield went to church on Sunday. The Irish Catholics went to Grenville for the nine o'clock mass at St. Brendan's. The priest there was enormously popular because he rattled his way through the mass in twenty-three minutes flat and never mentioned money. One faithful parishioner, Mary-Catherine MacGuire bragged, "Our kneelers fly and up and down so fast you're confessed, blessed and out on the steps before you know it."

The French-speaking Catholics made their way to Hawkesbury for the ten o'clock mass at St. Antoine de Padoue. The priest there was very entertaining. His knees cracked like pistol shots when he genuflected, and he drained all the wine from the chalice before the first note of the Sanctus had died away.

"He takes a drop or two more during the Agnus Dei," our neighbour Pierre Duclos told us with a grin, "One time he took so much that he sang the Gloria twice and forgot about the Kyrie altogether. We laughed 'til we pretty near died."

We Presbyterians followed the river road to Cushing for the eleven o'clock service at St. Paul's. Our minister, Reverend McIsaac was neither popular nor entertaining. He felt it his duty to preach sermons that went on for at least 45 minutes. He watched the collection plate like a hawk and if the takings were skimpy he sent it around again. Every move he made and every word he uttered was calculated to keep us off balance and he succeeded.

"Dear children, give me your full attention," he started off sweetly each Sunday morning. We looked up at him warily and braced ourselves for what might follow.

"The guid[4] Lord seeth all thy actions," he cooed in his Scottish burr. That remark certainly made us sit up and listen. Then he leaned over the pulpit and studied our worried faces.

His eyes narrowed and he bellowed, "Sloth!"

We thought of chores left undone and we trembled.

"False witness!" he hissed and we blushed at the fibs we'd told recently.

"Thievery!" he yelled triumphantly and we cringed because of the apples we'd pinched from our neighbours' trees. Beads of sweat broke out on our upper lips and we squirmed uneasily on the hard pews. Satisfied that we were thoroughly cowed, he turned his attention to the adults.

"Pa-r-rents," he began in his most reasonable voice, "you expect obedience from your bairns but are you obedient to the word of God?"

His beady eyes raked over the congregation and he answered the question himself by shrieking, "You are not!"

He paused to catch his breath and then screamed, "Consorting with Roman Catholics, playing cards, indulging in idle gossip. I'm aware of it all and what a shameful example you set for these pr-r-recious wee ones!"

Parents, grand-parents, neighbors and friends shifted in their seats and averted their eyes.

"And that's not all," he whispered menacingly. The men cleared their throats and the women coughed nervously.

They jumped when he yelled, "R-r-raffle tickets! I've haird[5] that some among you are buying r-r-raffle tickets. A Popish practice and one that will sh r-r-rivel your very soul."

[4] good
[5] heard

His thin lips tightened and his nostrils flared. He drew himself up to his full five feet, two inches to deliver his parting shot. He shook his fist and thundered, "The great abyss yawns before ye, and the flames of hell are lickin' at your heels. R-r-repent, before you're lost for-r-rever!"

He mopped his glistening forehead and smoothly changed gears.

"All stand to sing, 'Jesus Wants Me for a Sunbeam' following which the collection will be taken up," he purred, "and mind you be generous. The Lord loves a cheerful giver."

Shakily we all got to our feet, scared silly and wracked with guilt.

I guess that's why my sister Diane and I treasure the memory of one hilarious Sunday when the awful Reverend McIsaac was struck dumb and our brow-beaten congregation laughed like a band of happy heathens.

The Tuesday before, Reverend McIsaac called a meeting of the Ladies' Aid. Diane and I were recovering from chicken-pox, still too scabby to go out in public but not sick enough to be confined to bed.

"This is so inconvenient," Mum complained, "I can't miss today's meeting. Reverend McIsaac stressed that all the ladies must be there. What'll I do with you two?"

"Leave us here," Diane suggested, "We'll make fudge. I think I know how."

"What?" screeched Mum, "Leave you here and come back to find the house burned down and my best saucepan ruined? Absolutely not!"

"I'll have to take you with me," she decided, "The meeting's in the manse so you can wait in the Kirk. Just be quiet and stay out of sight."

Down at St. Paul's, Mum spirited us in through the side door and left us in the choir room with crayons and colouring books. The piano was shrouded in a dust sheet and the chairs were arranged in rows for Thursday night's choir practice.

"Look here," whispered Diane peeking under a cushion, "Cough drops, and the box is practically full. Here, have one."

Popping it under my tongue I sat down to colour but Diane wandered around the room restlessly.

"Wonder what's in the closet," she mused pulling the door open.

"Whadda ya know, choir gowns," she said mischievously. She shrugged one over her shoulders, climbed on top of the piano and began to sing, 'O, For the Wings of a Dove' in a falsetto voice.

Getting into the spirit I grabbed a gown too, and leaping from chair to chair belted out, 'Will Your Anchor Hold in the Storms of Life?' I flung my arms about to make the sleeves billow like the sails of a ship.

"Yours must be the biggest gown of the bunch," Diane laughed and then our eyes met. "Mrs. Van Loon," we squealed and laughed our heads off.

Mrs. Van Loon was the organist and choir director at St. Paul's. She was also the tallest and fattest person we had ever seen in our lives. When she first came to the church, Hamish McLean, the treasurer and the skinniest man in the congregation was very critical of her.

"She`s got arms as big as hams, and fingers like pork sausages," he sniffed, "One fine day she`ll pull the stops r-r-right out of the organ. What the r-r-repairs will cost I dr-r-read to think."

"Maybe so," Jimmy McGregor, the Clerk of Session put in, "but what worries me most is that she`s nae got[6] a drop of Scots blood in her. When she keeps time, she counts in Dutch! It's not decent."

Stewie Bell, the oldest and fiercest of all the men, set his jaw and disagreed, "Och aye, ye can blether all ye like, but I won't hear a word against the lass. She's a fine figure of a woman and her playing brings a bit o' life into the sairvices.[7] The last organist we had couldna get nobbut'[8] a pathetic wheeze out of that organ."

Anyway, Diane and I got fed up staying in the choir room in spite of having Mrs. Van Loon's enormous gown to entertain us. Inching the door open, Diane stuck her head out and looked up and down the hall.

"The coast is clear," she hissed, "C'mon on. We'll play Hide-and-Seek in the church."

The sanctuary was cold and the sun coming through the stained glass windows cast watery streaks of colour across the pews. It was as silent as the grave and twice as creepy. I shivered and tugged at Diane's sleeve.

"Let's go back. I don't like it in here," I begged.

Diane snorted and said," Don't be silly. There's lots of good hiding places. Count to twenty and then come and find me."

She twirled away down the center aisle and disappeared into the murk. I covered my eyes and whispered the numbers to myself.

"Ready or not, here I come," I called softly.

I headed for the balcony and checked under all the pews. No Diane. I came down and looked in the cloakroom beside the front door. A tweed cap hung forlornly on a hook but otherwise the place was empty.

---

[6] She doesn't have

[7] Services

[8] Couldn't get anything

That's when I heard a scraping sound coming from the opposite end of the church. My heart began to pound. I'd have to pass right by Reverend McIsaac's pulpit to investigate. The very idea was enough to freeze the blood in my veins.

I heard a dull clunk and a stifled, "Ouch!"

My eyes flew up to the gleaming row of organ pipes and I caught a flash of Diane's red sweater. Stealthily I tiptoed down the side aisle, inched past the dreaded pulpit and headed for the vestry. I slid silently into the tiny room. There were three doors facing me. I mouthed "Eeny, meeny, miny moe," and opened the door on my left. Bingo! There was the staircase leading to the organ loft. I groped my way up and paused on the last step.

"I know you're here but this isn't fair," I said loudly to Diane, "I can hardly see a thing. Why don't you give yourself up?"

No reply. There was a stack of books on the floor to my left and a heap of cardboard boxes on my right. Slivers of light gleamed faintly through the row of organ pipes in front of me. The air was dry and musty. I sneezed and heard a smothered laugh. I decided a surprise attack was the best way to flush Diane out of her hiding place. Without warning I threw myself across the boxes and yelled, "Gotcha!"

Diane screamed, shot up from her hiding place and fell over backwards, her arms and legs flailing madly. I lunged and grabbed her ankle but she slipped out of my grasp and fell backwards into the organ pipes. They shuddered at the impact and fell one after the other like giant dominoes. Some hit the floor with a clang, some with a ping and others with ringing bell-like tones. The noise was tremendous.

"That's torn it," Diane yelled, "The whole world must have heard that. We'll be skinned alive."

"Quiet," I bellowed, "Listen for a minute."

We strained our ears for the sound of voices or running feet. We heard nothing. I let my breath out and said, "I think we're okay. Probably everyone's still at the meeting."

"Help me up," Diane said crossly, "We'll have to figure how to put all these pipes back before Mum comes looking for us."

I looked uncertainly from the empty spaces to the array of pipes on the floor.

"How can we tell which one goes where?" I asked her.

She shrugged, "Haven't got a clue, but it can't be that hard. Let's start with the smallest one and work our way up."

The first pipe slid easily into place but it was the only one that did. The others either had to be wrestled into spots that were too small, or propped up in holes that were too big. Most of them listed drunkenly to one side or the other.

"What'll we do now?" I asked.

Diane eyed the cardboard boxes speculatively,

"Just what we need," she said, "They'll get us out of trouble."

We stuffed the gaps with strips of cardboard and steadied the shakiest pipes with a couple of heavy boxes.

"That's better, not perfect, but it'll do," said Diane studying them with her head on one side..

"Yeah, no one ever looks at them anyway," I said airily.

We scampered down the stairs, shot through the sanctuary and were sitting quietly in the choir room, colouring and sucking cough drops when Mum came to take us home. She looked at us suspiciously.

"How did you get so grubby? Were you crawling around on the floor?" she asked.

"Well, we shouldn't have done it, but we tried on a couple of choir gowns," Diane confessed, "And I don't think that closet's been dusted in the last hundred years."

She coughed and blew her nose like a trumpet for good measure. That night we scrubbed away the grimy evidence of our time in the organ loft and crawled into bed to rest our aching muscles.

The following Sunday Mum inspected our scabs and decided we were presentable enough to attend church. We walked sedately into the sanctuary and took our places. Folding our hands in prayer, Diane and I raised our eyes and studied the organ pipes.

"So far, so good," she whispered to me out of the corner of her mouth.

"Amen!" I breathed and sat back to wait for the service to begin. An expectant hush fell over the congregation.

The vestry door opened. Reverend McIsaac strode in and stood at the lectern. The choir filed past and took their places in the choir stalls. Mrs. Van Loon cleared the vestry door with very little room to spare and sailed majestically to the organ. She arranged her music, pulled out a few stops and raised her powerful arms in a graceful arc over the keys.

Reverend McIsaac glowered at the congregation and barked out the first order of the day, "All r-r-rise to sing number thairty two[9], 'Let Joy Be Unconfined.'

---

[9] Thirty-two

We opened our books and filled our lungs. Mrs. Van Loon's meaty hands crashed down on the keys and her size twelves stomped on the pedals.

The organ pipes wobbled and let out a shocking cacophony of sound. The discordant notes reverberated around us setting our teeth on edge and rattling our brains. Mrs. Van Loon screamed and turned bright red.

Reverend McIsaac, who had the misfortune to be standing right below the organ pipes clapped his hands over his ears and staggered back against the altar. The flower arrangement tipped over and water cascaded down the chancel steps. Reverend McIsaac's mouth opened and closed several times but no sound came out. His eyes glazed over and all the colour drained from his face. We watched with interest as he reeled past the baptismal font and fell face down behind the communion table.

Mrs. Van Loon was nothing if not determined so she decided to start over. She struck the keys with extra force as if to punish them for letting her down. With clenched teeth and furrowed brow she soldiered on, subjecting us to an unnerving symphony of impossible chords and clashing cadences. Some of the lower notes were downright rude. The children began to giggle. The women tittered into their hankies. The men couldn't hold back and suddenly a huge roar of laughter rose to the rafters and rolled around and around the sanctuary.

Mrs. Van Loon's hands fell from the keys and she laughed like a drain, wobbling back and forth on her little bench like an enormous jelly.

Diane and I didn't move a muscle. Mum stared at the organ pipes and then turned to look at our frozen faces. Her mouth began to twitch and she laughed so hard the tears rolled down her cheeks.

She never asked and we never told, but she knew all right; she knew!

Stones
Ancient slabs beneath my feet
Wobbly rocks that tip me into the water
Giant boulders that make me King of the Castle
Slivers of shale that I can skip across the water
My playthings.

Wind
Loud, harsh
Power, destruction, gentleness, life
Soothing, warming, buffeting, pushing
Soft, fragrant
Breath

Chapter 10

Truth and Consequences

When Mrs. Harding invited us for supper, Mum and Aunt Polly said, "We'd love to come," and they meant it. But Diane and I and Ross and Cheryl groaned.

"It's too far," protested Diane, "It's almost at Lock 6 for pity's sake."

"I'll get blisters on my heels before we're half way there," whined Ross.

Cheryl spoke in her most persuasive voice, "Auntie Dorothy, don't you remember when we went to see Mrs. Harding last summer, I got poison ivy? I don't think I should go anywhere near her place."

"That's true, Mum," I said brightly, "Cheryl should stay home and I should stay behind to keep her company."

Mum was not swayed, "It's only a mile up the road. The walk will do you good."

Looking as woebegone as she could, Diane sighed, "It's boring there. There's nothing to do."

"We were looking forward to a long cool swim this afternoon, but I suppose a walk in the burning sun won't actually kill us," I added.

Mum's patience wore thin, "That's enough! Mrs. Harding is all alone since her husband died. It was kind of her to invite us and it's our duty as neighbors to go, so there's an end to it."

Resigned to our fate, we scrubbed our faces, knees and elbows and put on our Sunday best. Sighing heavily, we trailed along behind Mum and Aunt Polly. We stopped to skip stones in the canal once in a while and even stretched out in the shade of a huge maple tree to rest for a while. Mum and Aunt Polly steamed ahead and arrived at Mrs. Harding's lane first. They motioned for us to get our skates on so we ran the last little distance and caught up to them still feeling very sorry for ourselves. "We're here now, so you better make up your minds to make the best of it," Aunt Polly said with a smile that didn't quite reach her eyes.

Mrs. Harding was watching for us from her back porch and as soon as she spied us, she waved and sang out joyfully, "Hello, hello. Come on in. It's so good to see you."

We were patient for the first half hour. The ladies chatted about this and that while we tried not to fidget. We cheered up when Mrs. Harding bustled away to get some refreshments. We ate the cookies and downed the milk she provided as quickly as we could within the bounds of good manners.

Ross wiped his milk moustache on his arm much to Aunt Polly's chagrin and asked, "May we be excused to go out and play?"

"Of course you can," said Mrs. Harding kindly.

"Such polite children," she murmured to our mums as we fled.

We decided to explore the barn. Until a couple of years ago it had been home to about 30 cows, two teams of horses and a beautiful collie dog. The hay mows overflowed and the grain bins were full to the top. Birds nested in the rafters and mice made scuffling noises in the straw. Now it was empty and silent. There wasn't even a stray cat wandering around. The walls had been white-washed and the concrete floor was scrubbed clean. It neither looked nor smelled like a barn.

"Remember when these stalls were all occupied?" asked Ross, "Mr. Harding had the biggest herd for miles around. You'd never know it now, would you?"

Cheryl said dramatically," I think I can hear the ghosts of the cows mooing, can't you?"

Right away Ross bellowed and pawed the ground. We laughed and the ghosts vanished.

"Look here," said Diane excitedly, "The names of the cows are still on the beams above the stalls."

We followed her as she walked along, squinting at the faded letters and reading aloud, "Daisy, Bossy, Maybelle and Bony."

Ross, Cheryl and I hooted with laughter, "Bony? No wonder she disappeared."

"Oops," she giggled," I guess it's Bonny."

Next we decided to look around the dairy. All we found were several milk cans standing in a row like so many forgotten soldiers. It was chilly and damp in the stone building so we raced out into the sunshine to warm up.

"Let's go see Mrs. Harding's pig," suggested Cheryl, "The sty's around back."

When we got there the sty was empty and the trough was clean as a whistle.

"Aw shucks, I don't think there's a living thing on this farm," said Diane glumly.

"There's nothing to do so let's talk about supper," I suggested.

"Good idea," Ross said, "Besides I'm getting really hungry. What d'you think we'll have?"

"I know it won't be corn on the cob because it's too early for that," Cheryl mused, "So I'll say it'll be bologna and fried potatoes."

Thinking back to last year's visit, I made my guess, "Mrs. Harding mentioned stew when we were here last year. She even gave Mum her recipe, so I bet she made that today."

Eyes shining, Diane breathed, "Wouldn't it be great if we had pancakes and maple syrup? I just love maple syrup and beets too, but not together of course," she added hastily as the rest of us gagged.

Mum's voice rang out from the back porch, "Supper's ready. Come and get it."

As soon as we reached the steps, Mum shook her finger at us and whispered,

"Remember what we've told you!"

We rolled our eyes and followed her inside to wash our hands, naughtily mouthing behind her back, "Eat what's put in front of you and mind your manners."

"I 'm so hungry I could eat a horse," Diane boasted.

"I'm so hungry, I could eat an elephant," Ross said smacking his lips.

Cheryl turned to me and said, "Mrs. Harding bakes great pies and cakes, so I don't care what we get first, do you?"

"Nope," I replied happily, "I can get anything down if I know dessert's coming."

Poor innocent children that we were, we had no inkling of the shock we were about to suffer. We took our places at the table and tucked our napkins under our chins.

Mrs. Harding came out of the kitchen proudly carrying a steaming platter and said, "Your visit is well-timed. My son Wayne came a while back to kill my pig."

"Goody," I whispered to Cheryl, "We're having roast pork. Maybe we'll get the crackling. That's the best part!"

As Mrs. Harding set the food on the table, we all stared --first at the plate and then at each other. It wasn't roast pork at all. It was blood pudding! The sausages lay in a pile big enough to feed an army. We were speechless.

None of us had ever eaten blood pudding but we knew what it was because the butcher once tried to convince our mums to buy some. We were horrified beyond belief when he proudly held up the links for their consideration.

"How d'you fancy some nice fresh blood pudding," he said persuasively, draping the revolting stuff across his rough hands like a length of fine silk.

"Blood? You want us to eat blood? " we squeaked in horror and hid behind our mums' skirts.

Much to our relief Mum and Aunt Polly shook their heads and answered in tandem, "Oh, not today, thanks all the same. A few slices of ham is really all we need."

But seated now in Mrs. Harding's dining room, there was nowhere to hide and no way to refuse the food on offer. Frantically we shot looks of silent appeal in Mum's direction. She shook her head imperceptibly and drew her eyebrows together fiercely. We knew that she meant, "Eat it or else!"

We turned to Aunt Polly. Her eyes were closed and she appeared to be praying. No help there. The appalling dish was handed round. I looked desperately for the smallest sausage I could find and dropped it with a shiver onto my plate. Yellow beans and lettuce from the garden rounded out the meal. Desperately we kids eyed each other, each one waiting for someone else to begin eating. I looked at Ross. Usually he could be counted on to eat anything, but his teeth were clenched. I did notice that his hands were moving, though. Slyly he slid his plate to the edge of the table and then clumsily dropped his fork on the floor. He made a great show of scrabbling around under the table to retrieve it.

Mrs. Harding dashed off to the kitchen for a clean one and that's when Ross whipped the blood pudding off his plate and stuffed it in his sock. Next I noticed that Diane had resorted to her old trick of packing morsels of the unwanted food in her cheeks. I knew that any minute now she would ask to be excused and trot to the outhouse to get rid of it.

I kicked Cheryl's foot under the table to get her attention but she ignored me. She waited until Mrs.Harding and Aunt Polly were talking and then she craftily tipped slivers of her sausage over the edge of her plate and hid them in her pockets.

I watched in awe as Mum methodically cut her blood pudding into little pieces and ate it. I shuddered and looked away. I prayed fervently that I would faint and come to in another time and place.

"Are you enjoying the blood pudding?" Mrs. Harding asked solicitously.

"It's lovely and fresh. Such a difference when it's home-made," Mum responded cagily.

"Do you put oatmeal in it when you make it?" Aunt Polly inquired in a strangled voice, trying to sound interested and failing completely.

"As a matter of fact I do," Mrs. Harding answered, only too eager to give further details,"Of course I always use the natural casing, you know, the intest --"

Mum hastily interrupted, "Your lettuce is lovely and sweet and the beans are wonderful too."

Her tactic didn't work. Ross' eyes bugged out and he turned slightly green, Cheryl stifled a squeal and gasped, "Intestines?"

Diane blanched. She hadn't recovered properly from the news about the oatmeal. She loathed it in any shape or form. Thinking about intestines was the blow that threatened to knock her out completely.

Articulating with difficulty through her bulging cheeks, Diane managed to croak, "May I leave the table? I need to go- uh, uh, you know."

"Why certainly, my dear. Run along," Mrs. Harding said kindly.

Aunt Polly struggled to choke down a morsel before saying nonchalantly, "My goodness, I do believe I ate too many cookies with my tea. I'm not very hungry. Here Dorothy, you can have my share. It would be a shame to waste it."

It was a testimony to the strength of their friendship that Mum accepted another sausage without a word. I chewed my vegetables slowly and carefully, taking as much time as I could. Finally I put my knife and fork down. The blood pudding lay untouched in the middle of my plate. I was defeated. I had no pockets in my dress like Cheryl. I just couldn't bring myself to store it in my cheeks like Diane and I wasn't wearing socks so I couldn't try Ross' stunt.

I looked Mrs. Harding straight in the eye and said, "I'm sorry, Mrs. Harding. I know you went to a lot of trouble to make this blood pudding, but I just can't eat it. I don't care for it."

Mrs. Harding smiled sympathetically and said, "Don't worry about it. I'm sorry you don't like it. Next time I'll be sure to have something you do like."

She picked up my plate and took it into the kitchen.

Mum wasn't so forgiving. She leaned across the table and whispered, "No dessert for you, my girl. You know the rule."

Mrs. Harding came back with dessert and Mum said firmly, "Sheila won't have dessert, Mrs. Harding."

Ross studied the ceiling. Diane decided to count the floorboards and Cheryl fiddled self-consciously with her dessert spoon. They didn't care about me and I knew it.

Tears of self-pity filled my eyes when Mrs. Harding handed them generous wedges of apple pie, fragrant with cinnamon and brown sugar and topped with a huge dollop of whipped cream.

I watched enviously as Ross scooped up the juicy apples. I had a pang of jealousy when I saw Diane licking golden flakes of pastry from the corner of her mouth. I felt utterly betrayed when Cheryl graciously accepted a second helping. Miserably, I counted the minutes until the meal ended.

Mrs. Harding refused our offer to help with the dishes.

"I'll enjoy washing up and thinking of the nice visit we had today," she said, "It's not often I get the chance to cook for other people."

We started for home. The long walk in the fading light was a silent one, and my resentment simmered with each step. It came to a rolling boil when we turned in at our gate.

"I saw right through all your tricks, even if Mrs. Harding didn't," I yelled angrily at Ross, Diane and Cheryl.

"I had to do it. It was cruel to serve pig's blood mixed with oatmeal," Diane wailed, "I would've had nightmares for years if I'd swallowed that stuff."

"I'm delicate," Cheryl bawled, "That blood pudding would've finished me off so I had to protect myself."

"Blood is for vampires," Ross shouted pulling the sausage out of his sock and waving it in my face, "I might've ended up with eye teeth a foot long if I'd eaten this thing."

Furiously I screamed, "You're a bunch of sneaks, that's what you are. At least I told the truth."

"Big deal," Diane sneered, "You just couldn't think of anything clever to do like we did."

"Yeah," Ross agreed, "and besides, what did telling the truth get you?"

"No dessert! That's what," Cheryl said flatly, folding her arms across her chest.

Whoever said the truth hurts, knew what they were talking about.

Chapter 11

Mrs. MacNeil

Sometimes after chores were done and the supper dishes cleared away, Mrs. MacNeil walked the half-mile from the farm where she lived with her husband and came to join us on the Byrne's verandah.

She murmured, "Evening," to Mr. and Mrs. Byrne before sitting down in the nearest empty chair but she had no greeting for anyone else. Mrs. Mac-Neil was small and grim-looking. Her dark eyes glared at the world through wire-rimmed spectacles. Her gray hair was pulled back severely into a knot at the nape of her neck and no-nonsense hairpins kept every stray wisp firmly in place. Years of hard physical work had made her arms very muscular and her thick square hands were reddened and rough. She was so firmly corseted that she creaked when she moved. No matter how hot it was she wore coarse brown stockings and heavy black shoes, laced up and tied in double knots. The only thing that ever varied in her appearance was the colour of her cotton housedress which was always stiffly starched and perfectly ironed.

As soon as she sat down, she pulled out a package of Players' cigarettes and lit up. She gazed off into the distance as our talk and laughter ebbed and flowed around her. She never joined in. In fact she didn't even seem to be listening. Her gold wedding band glinted in the fading light as she lifted her smoke up and down. When her cigarette was finished, she tossed the butt over the verandah, nodded to Mr. and Mrs. Byrne and left.

Most nights she trudged straight back to her farm, but if it happened to be a Saturday night, she headed across the road to the Bar X Hotel and worked in the kitchen until closing time.

I pictured her washing tray after tray of beery glasses while in the background, cowboy songs wailed about lonely nights and love gone wrong. What did she think about as she plunged her work-worn hands into yet another sinkful of steaming hot water? Did she speak to anyone or was she as silent as she was with us? Was she scared walking home in the dark in the wee hours of the morning?

My questions were never answered because I never dared to ask them. There was a cloak of silence around Mrs. MacNeil so heavy that it smothered even my childish curiosity.

Forty years later the cloak was lifted when Mrs. MacNeil died and Maeve told me her story.

She began by revealing that Mrs. MacNeil's name was Fiona. That startled me. Such a gentle name for such a hard-looking woman. She told me that Fiona had been a beauty in her day, with long, wavy hair and laughing brown eyes. She caught the eye of Ewan MacNeil at a dance one January night when she was 20 years old. He made up his mind then and there to marry her. He swept her off her feet, taking her to every skating party, square dance and church social in the district. He was attentive and charming. They announced their engagement in May and were married in October. By Christmas, Fiona knew she had made a terrible mistake. Ewan's sweet words had turned into shouts. He was mean and rough with her. She worked hard in the house and on the farm to try and please him but his temper worsened with each passing year. Fiona's bright eyes dulled and her smile vanished. She seldom left the farm and Ewan discouraged anyone from visiting. Two boys were born and that didn't improve Ewan's temper one little bit.

"It'll be a long time before they can work. Until then they're just two more mouths to feed," he growled.

When a daughter arrived, he was furious, "Girls is nothing but trouble. Not strong enough to do any real work and always talking and going on about nothing."

But Fiona delighted in her little daughter. She named her Jeannie and found pleasure in her pretty ways and sweet nature.

If Ewan was working in a field far from the house or gone to town for supplies, then Fiona scooped Jeannie up and hurried away to visit Mrs. Byrne.

After a cup or two of strong tea and a hot buttered scone, Fiona's stony expression softened and she began to talk. She asked for news of her former friends and listened wistfully as Mrs.Byrne told her about recent card parties or church suppers.

When Fiona rose to go, Mrs. Byrne gave Jeannie a kiss and patted Fiona affectionately on the shoulder, "Come again, Fiona. Our door is always open to you and darling Jeannie."

Year after dreary year, Fiona watched as the boys slaved alongside their father getting nothing but curses and blows for their efforts. Day after day, she listened as Ewan berated Jeannie for being a useless female. Anything Fiona said or did in defense of her children only made Ewan angrier.

Things came to a head one bright summer morning when Jeannie was about thirteen years old. As usual Fiona cooked a pot of porridge for breakfast. Jeannie helped dish it up and carried the bowls to the table. Ewan sat in stony silence as the jug of cream was passed around. Jeannie had poured only a couple of drops onto her porridge when Ewan lunged across the table and struck her such a blow on the head that she fell off her chair.

"Where do you get off taking that much cream for your porridge?" he bellowed, "By rights you shouldn't have any at all for all the work you do around here."

He ran around the table and kicked her as she cowered on the floor and called her every awful name under the sun. The two boys jumped on Ewan's back and wrestled him away from their sister. Fiona shouted to Jeannie, "Run, Jeannie, run. Go to Mrs. Byrne and stay there."

Jeannie did as her mother said, stumbling across the fields, tears pouring down her cheeks and her heart nearly bursting out of her chest. Sobbing with pain and shock, she practically fell through the screen door into the sunny kitchen where Mrs. Byrne was just about to pour the tea for her husband and daughter.

"You're all right now Jeannie," Mrs. Byrne said over and over as she cradled her in her arms, "I've got you. You're all right."

Over the next few days, Jeannie confided in Mr. and Mrs. Byrne and Maeve. Bitterly she revealed the extent of the misery that her father inflicted on her and her brothers and her mother.

"Did your parents call the police?" I asked Maeve.

Maeve shook her head and explained, "In those days, the police didn't get involved in family matters. A man could do what he liked to his wife and children, short of killing them outright. He owned them just like he owned his cattle.

"So nothing ever happened to Ewan," I said flatly, horrified at the thought.

She winked at me and smiled, "Not exactly. When Ewan came back to the house that day after the evening milking, he found my parents waiting for him. Mother and Dad never would tell me what passed between them, but Jeannie lived with us until she was old enough to strike out on her own. Fiona visited her every day but Ewan never darkened the door of our place again."

"What about the boys and Mrs. MacNeil?" I asked.

"Ewan never laid a finger on the boys after that day but they left home as soon as they could," Maeve said soberly.

"They kept in touch with their mother and tried to persuade her to leave Ewan and live with them but for some reason she never did," Maeve said shaking her head.

The memory of Mrs. MacNeil's brooding eyes and silent ways came flooding back and my heart ached for her sadness and her silence.

Chapter 12

Minnie's Gift

Every summer, Mum and Aunt Polly made sure we called on all the neighbors within walking distance. These visits were a lot of fun if there were kids for us to play with. We jumped in their haylofts, played with their dogs and followed them to their secret hideouts in the woods. Often we were treated to a slice of homemade pie or cake or even a meal, but the visit to Minnie's place didn't have any of those attractions.

To begin with she had no kids, no hayloft and no dogs. What she did have was a pesky cow who managed to corner us and lick our legs with her rough tongue until we screamed for help.

"Dainty only wants to say hello," Minnie would say fondly, puzzled by our shrieks of alarm.

There wasn't room for us to run around either. Her property was so overgrown that we had to push our way through the branches of an apple tree gone wild, a huge patch of nettles and a forest of hollyhocks just to get within shouting distance of her front door. Her house was so crooked that everyone except Minnie expected it to collapse whenever a storm blew in from the northeast. It had been built of rough lumber and left for 70 years or so to acquire what colour it could from the elements. It boasted two doors. The front one looked sturdy enough but it was never used. The back door was in a dreadful state but that's the one everyone used. It sagged on its hinges and the screen bulged like an old balloon. Even the noise of it closing was more of an exhausted sigh than a slam.

This lethargy crept from the house to the yard where a narrow path meandered from the stable to the outhouse and on to the well before it petered out completely a few yards away from a frayed clothesline. Not that it mattered since Minnie never hung up her washing. She preferred to spread her bits and pieces over the low shrubs that crowded around her back door.

"Not so far to walk, my dears," she explained to us one day, "Anyway, having my clothes flap about in the wind might damage them."

Moth-eaten and threadbare as they were, we agreed that a gentle nap on a bush was safer. Anyhow, on the day I have in mind, when Mum and Aunt Polly announced were we were going to visit Minnie, we weren't best pleased.

"We're going and that's flat, so don't bother whining," they said, "Wash your knees and elbows, not just your hands and faces before we go."

"And don't speak until you're spoken to," we chorused before they did.

We complained bitterly as we fought our way past the apple tree, the nettles and the hollyhocks. On the other side of that jungle we were pleasantly surprised to find ourselves facing waves of black-eyed susans and billows of wild blue asters. We stopped to catch our breath and enjoy the view before tackling the final leg of our journey to Minnie's back door.

We waited while Mum knocked and called out, "Hello Minnie. Are you at home to visitors today?"

Minnie shuffled to the door wearing brown plaid slippers and a tattered fawn sweater. Thick cotton stockings bagged around her ankles and the uneven hem of her dress trailed here and there on the floor.

Not many people visited Minnie but she knew how to treat guests all the same. She pushed open the shaky door and fluttered her hand in a welcoming motion.She had smooth unlined skin but her sweet smile revealed an unfortunate gap where her four top teeth should have been.

"I'm so pleased to see you," she lisped, "I wasn't expecting callers and I've not had time to tidy up, but never mind."

One by one we stepped over the door-sill and followed Minnie into the kitchen. It was a muffled procession as Minnie's house had the distinction of being the only one in Stonefield with earth floors.

Gesturing at a chipped enamel basin on the table, Minnie explained, "As you can see, I was just doing my lunch dishes. Sit down and make yourselves at home. I'll be finished in a jiffy."

We looked imploringly at our mothers because the chairs were already occupied by an assortment of mangy cats, a decrepit basket holding six eggs and a dented pan half-full of corn for the hens.

Using raised eyebrows and subtle shakes of her head, Aunt Polly directed us to a relatively uncluttered bench. With Cheryl and me perched on our mothers' laps and Ross and Diane wedged in between, we all managed to sit down. Minnie resumed her task. Slowly she swished her dish mop back and forth in the scummy water. Now and again she dipped her fingers into the murky depths to fish out a fork or a spoon. She left everything spread out haphazardly on the table to dry and wiped her hands on a grubby towel before settling into a wobbly rocking chair. She seemed perfectly comfortable although I know for a fact she was sitting on a ball of binder twine and a curry comb.

"Another job done," she said with a contented sigh, "Now tell me all your news."

Mum and Aunt Polly chattered brightly to Minnie while we kids studied the room. It was so untidy that we weren't too sure what we were looking at. Articles of clothing drooped from every piece of furniture, mixed up with what looked like bits of leather tack for a horse. A rusty trowel and a china vase sat cheek by jowl on the dresser while piles of crockery teetered on stacks of musty books. An ancient nightdress was draped modestly around Minnie's butter churn.

If the walls had ever had a lick of paint, there was no trace of it left. Years of wood smoke and neglect had darkened them to a nondescript brown. The low ceiling matched the drabness of the walls. The smell in the room was hard to identify. Many of the houses in Stonefield bore a whiff of the barn, which didn't bother us a bit, and we liked the yeasty smell of baking bread or the sharp tang of laundry soap. But here in Minnie's kitchen, the air was musty and we wrinkled our noses.

Mum noticed and suggested a tour of the garden. Minnie's garden smelled fresh but it was just as disorganized as her kitchen. Gorgeous flowers bloomed alongside ordinary vegetables. Feathery carrot tops and sweet-faced pansies tickled our ankles at one and the same time. Queen Anne's Lace nodded regally over a straggly row of yellow beans. I'm sure I saw onions standing to attention among a froth of buttercups.

Gazing happily at the riotous growth around her, Minnie pointed out various plants with all the pride of a loving mother.

"Now children," she urged, "Come and stand near me so you can have a really close look at my brave little marigolds. They protect my parsley and my turnips from all kinds of nasty bugs, you know."

Directing our gaze a little farther ahead, Minnie spoke with a tinge of exasperation in her voice, "Oh dear, look at Sweet William. He's so naughty. I never know from one day to the next where he's going to pop up."

Lowering her voice, she spoke confidentially, "He's inclined to be a teensy bit willful, you know. He likes to take over. Not like my lovely Mallow here. No, all she asks for is a drop of rain and her fair share of sunshine and she blooms and blooms."

We realized that we could be in Nellie's garden for a very long time. No neat hedge or picket fence defined its borders and Minnie showed no signs of tiring. Diane wiggled her eyebrows at Cheryl and me, sending a silent appeal to find a way to get us out of there.

"Thank-you for showing us your flow--your vege----your, your garden, Minnie," Cheryl said in a breathy rush.

We started to move away but Aunt Polly suddenly knelt down and cupped her hands around some delicate pink lilies. She pushed back the choking tendrils of a cucumber plant and inquired, "How did these lilies ever get here, Minnie?"

"Oh my," tittered Minnie, "There's quite a story to tell about them."

"Let me see," she mused, "Where should I begin? I think it was the middle of September when my cousin Reg dropped in for a little visit. No, I tell a lie. It was the first week of October. I remember now because it was my birthday. Reg gave me a present of some bulbs."

Minnie's brown eyes sparkled as she went on, "I was ever so pleased. I put them on the floor in the kitchen near the west window until I could decide where to store them for the winter. What with one thing and another, I quite forgot about them."

She turned to Mum and Aunt Polly with a frown and appealed to them for understanding, "There's always so much to do, isn't there, to keep a house running smoothly? Especially through the winter months. Don't you find?"

They nodded in complete accord.

Her worried look vanished and she laughed, "Then one day in May I decided to sweep the kitchen floor and that's when I found the bulbs right where I'd left them all those months ago."

"Only thing was," she whispered now as if sharing a wonderful secret, "They'd started to grow. They had actually taken root in the floor of my kitchen. What do you think of that?"

Aunt Polly had a sudden coughing fit so Mum answered Minnie's question, "Well, they must have got a great start in your kitchen floor, Minnie, because they're beautiful."

Minnie beamed and said, "Thank-you. Now you must come back to the house for a cup of tea. I might even be able to find a biscuit for the children."

"We wouldn't dream of putting you to the trouble," Mum said hastily.

"Oh, no thanks, Minnie," added Aunt Polly, "It's time for the children to go for a swim before supper."

Minnie thought for a moment and then said, "Well if you can't stay for tea, then I'll send you home with a little something instead. Follow me."

Scurrying to the well, Minnie leaned down and pulled up a stoneware crock. We crowded around as she lifted the lid. It was full to the top with pale yellow butter. Beads of moisture shimmered across the surface like pearls on a string. In the center Minnie had stamped an attractive thistle design.

Minnie hitched the heavy crock a little higher and spoke with surprising authority, "Feast your eyes on this butter. I churned it with my own two hands. You know, when you buy butter in the shops you have no idea who made it, do you? Why, it could come from anywhere couldn't it?"

We'd never thought of that. Nodding anxiously, we kids agreed.

"When you spread this on your bread tonight, you'll have no worries because you'll know it came from Dainty and me," she said proudly.

Tilting her head to one side, she dreamily traced over the thistle with one grubby finger. Mum and Aunt Polly said they couldn't possibly accept such a generous gift but Minnie responded swiftly, "Nonsense, it's the least I can do for such good neighbors. I want you to have it."

Aunt Polly winced when Minnie retrieved the lid from the ground and placed it on top of the dish. A few wisps of dry grass stuck out here and there.

"Well, if you insist," said Mum weakly.

"It's very kind of you," murmured Aunt Polly, "It looks absolutely delicious."

We left Minnie standing by the well basking in the warmth of the compliment.

As soon as we got home Mum washed the outside of the crock with a hot soapy cloth and put it in the ice-box. When we sat down for supper, there was no butter on the table.

Holding a slice of bread in one hand and his knife in the other, Ross asked, "So where's Minnie's butter?"

Mum said firmly, "We won't be eating Minnie's butter."

Ross laid down his knife with a clatter.

"Why not?" he squawked.

Diane said mutinously, "I'm not eating that awful margarine."

"I want Minnie's butter. I love butter," Cheryl whined.

"Minnie wanted us to have it. She said so," I added.

"Maybe she did but we're not going to eat it," Aunt Polly insisted, "Think of the state of her kitchen. It's not safe to eat anything that comes out of there."

Ross asked, "But what are you going to do with it?"

Mum leaned across the table and whispered hoarsely, "Bury it!"

I couldn't believe my ears.

"Bury it?" I echoed.

"What'll you say if Minnie asks if we ate it?" Diane asked.

Mum cleared her throat and dropped another bomb, "Well, we won't tell her the whole truth exactly."

"There are ways of bending the truth a little when it's necessary," Aunt Polly added.

"Humph! Sounds to me like you're gonna tell a lie," Ross said skeptically and ducked before Aunt Polly could smack him.

That night, as soon as it was dark, Mum and Aunt Polly took the crock of butter, a large spade and a small flashlight and crept out to the darkest corner of our garden. They dug a deep hole, dumped Minnie's butter into it and mounded the earth firmly overtop.

A week later, they baked a large pan of shortbread. When it was cool, they cut it up and packed it in Minnie's empty crock.

"Polly and I are going to return Minnie's crock," said Mum, "You can come along but don't you dare say a word about the butter. I'll do the talking."

When we got there, Minnie was moving around in her garden, stopping now and then to trail her hand over a particularly lush tomato or bury her nose in an especially fragrant flower. Dainty was chewing her cud in the shade of the apple tree. We eyed her warily and kept our distance.

Mum called out," Yoo-hoo, Minnie. We're here to return your crock."

Aunt Polly placed the crock in Minnie's hands and said, "We baked a little something for you to say thank-you for your butter."

Minnie lifted the lid and smiled broadly, "Shortbread," she exclaimed, "My favourite!"

She took a big sniff and sighed with pleasure.

"Did you use my butter to make it by any chance?" she asked eagerly.

We kids were all ears when Mum opened her mouth.

"Why Minnie, "she said, "Polly and I couldn't possibly make shortbread like that without using the very best butter, could we?"

We left Minnie still standing amongst her flowers and cradling the crock of shortbread in her arms. She looked like the happiest woman in the world.

That man talks so much
My head aches.
Mrs. Byrne is right
Empty bags make the biggest bangs.

Forlorn
The swing
Dangles from the Butternut tree
Waiting for me
To take it on a journey
To heaven and back
On the wings of my laughter
Happy

Chapter 13

Divine Justice

In the summer of 1950 Ross and Cheryl and Diane and I were enthralled by Roy Rogers and Dale Evans. We walked like them, talked like them and sang the songs they sang in their movies. That's why we were goggle-eyed when our friend Billy told us his big news.

He was leaning up against a ramshackle shed at the time with his straw hat tipped low over his eyes. He hitched up his overalls, chewed on a stalk of hay and tried to look nonchalant.

"My dad sez I can fix this place up like a bunkhouse," he said casually.

"A bunkhouse? Ya mean like where cowboys sleep when they're not out ridin' the range?" squeaked Cheryl.

"Yup," he drawled," An' I 'spect this'll be exackly like the one on Roy Rogers' ranch when I get done with it."

Diane studied the junk lying around and tapped the broken floorboards with the toe of her shoe. Doubt was written all over her face, "It'll take some doin'. 'Course, we could pitch in and help if you want."

Billy stroked his chin, "Waal, I reckon it's a job jis' for guys, but if you're sure…"

Diane, Cheryl and I burst out, "Whadda ya mean, jis' for guys? We can work as hard as guys any day."

"Tell you what then," Billy responded generously, "Ross an' I'll go build a coupla bunks while you three gals start cleanin'."

The next hour turned out to be pretty tough. Our brooms raised clouds of choking dust. A large family of mice scampered over our feet when we discovered their nest under a pile of feed sacks. Spiders as big as doorknobs dangled from the ceiling and garter snakes slithered through the cracks in the floorboards.

"Don't you dare scream," Diane warned Cheryl and I as yet another horror wiggled past, "Or the guys'll tease us no end."

Gritting our teeth, Cheryl and I soldiered on.

Eventually Ross and Billy appeared, dragging a rickety bunkbed. There were a few muttered swear words and a horrible scraping sound as they forced it through the doorway.

"Lookit that," said Billy proudly, "Ever' bit as good as the ones on Roy's ranch."

"That's fer doggone sure," Ross agreed.

"The cowboys'll 'preciate having someplace nice to sleep when they come in from the round-up tonight," said Billy.

"We sure will," agreed Diane enthusiastically.

"I'm an ole cowhand, from the Rio Grande," sang Cheryl, while Diane whirled an imaginary lasso. I jingled my invisible spurs and tipped my pretend ten-gallon hat over my eyes. Any minute now, I expected Roy and Dale to come through the door, so it was a bit of a letdown when Ross said it was time to go home for supper.

"We're having fun. Let's stay for a while longer," begged Diane, "Besides, we've gotta decide what we're gonna bring back for the night."

"Yeah, that's right," added Cheryl, "D'you want us to bring some chow?"

Billy and Ross exchanged looks.

"Heck no,"said Billy, "This here bunkhouse is jis' for us guys. Girls ain't welcome in a bunkhouse!"

Diane asked angrily, "D'you mean you're not gonna let us sleep here jis' 'cause we're girls?"

"Fraid so," Billy replied.

"You gotta be tough to sleep in a bunkhouse. Girls jis' don't have what it takes," Ross explained earnestly.

"You dirty, lowdown varmints," Diane snarled, "You got us to work for you and then you won't let us sleep here. You're a couple of stinkers."

"Yeah, stinkers," Cheryl and I echoed indignantly.

If we were counting on a sympathetic hearing from our mothers when we got home, we didn't get it.

"Surely you can see that it wouldn't be proper for you girls to sleep in some filthy old shed with the boys," Mum said.

"I can't think why you would even want to," Aunt Polly went on, "There must be all sorts of creatures roaming around there at night."

"It's not a shed, it's a real bunkhouse," Cheryl cried, "And it's every bit as clean as the one on Roy and Dale's ranch. We worked like dogs sweepin' and scrapin' to get it jis' right."

"It's not fair that Ross gets to go jis' 'cause he's a boy!" I protested.

Mum looked at us over her glasses, a sure sign she wasn't convinced.

"You don't understand," Diane wailed and tried to explain how badly we wanted to sleep in a real bunkhouse.

"What would your dads say if we let you sleep there?" asked Mum.

"We don't care," we howled.

"What would the neighbours say?" asked Aunt Polly.

"We don't care," we hollered.

When Mum folded her arms across her chest we knew we were beat.

Jealously, we watched Ross get ready for his night in the bunkhouse. He slung a blanket over his shoulder and rolled his pyjamas up in a towel. Then he filled a paper bag with cookies and soft drinks.

We heard him humming, 'Happy Trails to You,' as the screen door slammed behind him.

"I hope there's a big storm tonight," said Cheryl through clenched teeth, "Ross is afraid of thunder."

"I hope bats fly in and get tangled in his hair," Diane snarled.

"I hope the mice all come back," I said in my meanest voice, "Billy's scared stiff of them.

"Would you girls like to play checkers?" asked Mum brightly.

"No!"

"How about Go Fish?" Aunt Polly suggested.

"No!"

We held out until they offered us hot chocolate and toast. As we sipped and crunched, we moaned about all the fun we were missing.

"I bet they're singing cowboy songs right now," Cheryl said wistfully.

Diane sighed, "They're prob'ly getting ready for their midnight feast."

"Maybe Roy and Dale have dropped in," I whimpered.

"Never mind all that," said Mum briskly, "It's time you were in bed. Things will look better in the morning. They always do."

We hadn't been asleep for very long when we were wakened by the sound of someone pounding on our front door. Mum leaped out of bed and flew downstairs with Aunt Polly hard on her heels.

"Let me in," the voice screamed, "Hurry! Oh, ow! I think I'm dyin'."

Petrified, we huddled behind Mum. The yelling got even louder.

"Open up! Open up."

"Whoever can it be?" asked Mum. "I've never heard such a racket."

"Don't open the door," warned Cheryl, "It could be an outlaw!"

"Maybe it's a cattle rustler," I suggested helpfully.

"In the name of God, let me in," begged the voice.

"Wait a sec, that sounds like Ross," said Diane, "Listen!"

"Help me, I'm near done for. Open up, pleeeze! Ma, are you there?" he pleaded.

"That is Ross," gasped Aunt Polly, "Quick, open the door."

Mum turned the key and the door swung back. An overpowering stench of skunk enveloped us like a tidal wave.

"Ew, ew, what a stink!" yelled Diane holding her arm across her face. Cheryl and I gagged and pinched our noses.

"Ross is that you?" gasped Aunt Polly, "Ross? Take that towel off your head and answer me."

Ross unwrapped his head and stood shivering miserably in the damp night air while the smell grew in intensity.

"What the deuce happened to you?" Mum asked, quite unnecessarily I thought.

"Jis' let me in and I'll explain," Ross implored her. We shrank back against the wall as he stumbled over the doorsill.

Mum gulped and held her nose, "I'll jusd rud and see if we've god any domado juice in the pandry. Go indo the kidchen and for goodness' sake, doan douch anythig."

We watched from a safe distance while Aunt Polly and Mum stood him in the laundry tub and scrubbed him down with a dishmop dunked in a basin of tomato juice.

"Ow, Ow, Ow," he screamed, "That stuff's freezin!"

"Can't be helped," Mum said as she poured the last can of juice over his head, "Tell us what happened."

Shivering and whimpering, Ross told his sorry tale.

"Billy and I sang some songs for a while and then we had our midnight snack. Everything was goin' great. Then we decided to practice some roping," he sputtered through the juice that was dripping from his hair.

"First I was the cowboy and Billy was the calf. I lassoed him and tied him up good."

He licked his lips, made a terrible face and continued, "Then Billy was the cowboy and I was the calf. We rassled so hard the whole place was shaking. All of a sudden, those dumb bunks come away from the galldarned wall. Billy fell on top of me and the bunks came down on the top of the both of us. Boys howdy, that Billy sure can holler! I think that's what got the skunks so mad. Before we knew what was goin' on they came out from under the floor and sprayed us."

Ross wailed, "My eyes stung so bad I couldn't hardly see."

He swallowed hard and sobbed, "Billy got sprayed even worse'n me. He ran cryin' to his Ma. She was hoppin' mad and wouldn't let him nor me in the house. She told us to wash ourselves off in the creek and go sleep in the barn."

Diane, Cheryl and I began to laugh. Joy filled our little girlish hearts. We had learned in Sunday school that justice would roll down like a mighty river and here was the proof. No matter that the river was actually a few squirts of skunk oil. We thanked God anyway and burst into song:

"The stars at night, are big and bright,
Deep in the heart of Texas.
The sage in bloom, is like perfume,
Deep in the heart of Texas."
"Hang on," Diane screeched, "Shouldn't that be…"
"The stars at night, are big and bright
Shinin' down on Bill's ole bunkhouse.
The skunks sashayed and then they sprayed.
So now it's just a stinkhouse!"

She came uninvited
An uncomfortable person
"I knew this house before you came," she said.
"You changed the wallpaper."
"What a shame!"
"Only twenty years old
and as good as the day it was licked up."

Chapter 14

Cattle Rustlers

Every Saturday afternoon Mum and Aunt Polly dropped us kids off at the movie theater in Hawkesbury and went shopping. They usually started out at Betnetski's hardware for paraffin wax and jam jars before moving on to Mr. Apelbaum's drugstore for shampoo and soap. Mr. Vogel's Drygoods Emporium was one of their favourite haunts because Mrs. Vogel was so friendly and full of news. A refreshing cup of tea and a slice of pie at Fred's Café gave them the strength to cross the street to the A&P to buy their groceries.

Meanwhile, we kids were galloping across the Wild West with the likes of Roy Rogers, Wild Bill Hickok and the Lone Ranger. For two thrilling hours, we fired guns with the outlaws, roped cattle with the cowboys and whooped with the Indians.

I recall one Saturday in particular. Gene Autry's latest movie, 'Cow Town', was the main attraction and we were completely enthralled. Even before the credits began to roll we had decided to stage our own version of it. As soon as we got home, we scrambled up the apple tree and argued about who would be the cowboys and who would get to be the rustlers.

On Sunday we decided on costumes and looked around the house for props so when Monday morning rolled around we were ready to ride the range. We came down for breakfast dressed in blue jeans and plaid shirts with cotton handkerchiefs knotted around our necks.

"Why are you dressed like that?" Mum asked, "It's eighty in the shade!"

As planned, Ross, Cheryl and I looked nonchalant while Diane answered for all of us, "We're going to check Monsieur Lemay's wood-lot for you, to see if the raspberries are ripe. It's full of burrs and thorns in there and we don't want to get scratched."

"Good thinking," Aunt Polly said, "If the berries are ready, we'll go up there first thing tomorrow before the birds get to them."

Mum and Aunt Polly went into the pantry to count jam jars and bags of sugar.

I think making jam was their favorite pastime. While I acted as look-out, Diane ducked out the back door and quietly took down the washing line. Cheryl eased the string mop out of the broom cupboard and Ross slipped his cap gun inside his shirt. We crept out the back door and ran off at break-neck speed keeping a steady pace until we reached Monsieur Lemay's wood-lot. We took a quick look at the raspberries and went on to our real destination, Monsieur Lemay's cow pasture. His prize herd of Holsteins raised their heads and watched curiously as we clambered over the fence.

"Cheryl," Ross directed, "You're one of the cowboys looking after the herd so get on your horse and ride around. Sing something to keep them calm."

Obediently Cheryl straddled her mop and loped westward warbling, 'I'm an Ole Cowhand from the Rio Grande.'

"Your turn, Sheila," Ross said, giving me a shove, "You're riding the range with Cheryl. Take it slow and don't look back. I'll be Gene and Diane will be Tex. We're gonna sneak up and rustle them thar cows right out from under your noses."

Grasping imaginary reins I galloped off. The cows blinked at Cheryl and me a few times, then went back to snatching mouthfuls of grass. Diane looped the washing line into a lasso and walked slowly towards the cows.

Ross pulled out his gun, dropped in a roll of caps, sucked in his breath and screamed, "Geronimo! Let's go get'em, Tex!"

The cows looked up and stopped chewing. Diane rushed at them from one side, twirling her lasso wildly in the air. Ross charged them from the opposite side, firing his gun and yelling "Gee haw," at the top of his lungs.

"Git away from our cattle, you lowdown dirty rustlers," Cheryl screeched, and forgetting that her mop was supposed to be a horse, she began swinging it above her head. The cows began to mill around uneasily. Diane's rope whistled through the air and snaked across their backs. That really spooked them. They stamped their feet, lashed the air with their tails and tossed their heads. Ross stopped to reload his gun but the cows didn't stick around to hear him fire it.

The entire herd thundered to the far end of the field, snorting and bawling loud enough to wake the dead. They were so frightened their eyes rolled back in their heads.

Cheryl and I kept on hootin' and hollerin' while Ross tore after the cows firing one roll of caps after another. The terrified animals lumbered around and around the field until their tongues lolled out of their mouths and their sides were streaked with sweat.

Suddenly one of them sagged to her knees and rolled over onto her back wheezing and slobbering. Her hooves pedaled the air feebly.

"Gee, you must have made her run too hard, Ross," Cheryl said pointing at the prostrate animal.

"Could be," he said uncertainly, "But in the movie they stampeded for ages and none of them keeled over like that."

"Aw shucks, that cow must be weak or something. Too bad, just when things were going so great," Diane said, sounding put out.

"If Mr. Lemay finds her like this, he'll be mad," I said, "I think we should get out of here pronto!"

"Yeah, maybe we should," Cheryl agreed, "Although he won't come to get the cows 'til after four o'clock and by then she'll prob'ly be fine."

"Anyways we can come back in a day or two and play again. It'll be even better next time," Ross said confidently.

Diane gathered up her rope, Ross pocketed his gun, Cheryl slung the mop over her shoulder and we headed home congratulating each other all the way for such a great game, even though we had to cut it short.

When we trooped into the house Diane sang out, "There's tons of raspberries, Mum."

The next day Mum and Aunt Polly polished up their berry pails and set out for Monsieur Lemay's raspberry patch. They were back in 20 minutes with no berries and steam practically coming out of their ears.

"What's the matter?" Ross asked.

"Monsieur Lemay was guarding his place with a rifle, if you can believe it. He wouldn't let us anywhere near his berry patch. Said he had to protect his land and his cattle," Aunt Polly said scornfully, "He called us trespassers, if you can imagine anything so silly. Why, we've been neighbors for years and he's always let us pick raspberries in his woodlot."

Diane and I eyed each other nervously and Cheryl cleared her throat a couple of times before asking, "What else did he say, exactly?"

Mum plunked her empty berry pail on the table and said, "Some malarkey about his pasture getting all torn up and one cow laid out cold."

"He claimed his herd was so upset that he couldn't get a drop of milk out of them at the evening milking, " Aunt Polly added, " And boy, was he peeved about that!"

Mum continued, "You should've heard him ranting. He actually thinks there were cattle rustlers around here yesterday. Polly and I nearly burst out laughing."

Diane snickered, "Rustlers? Here? In Stonefield?"

"Sounds to me like he's been watching too many cowboy movies," Ross said.

"I don't think Monsieur Lemay has time to go to many movies," Mum said drily.

"No," she went on, "Something happened all right, but exactly what, I don't know."

We kids sidled out the door and shinnied up the apple tree.

"Did you hear what they said? Monsieur Lemay thinks there were rustlers," Ross guffawed, "And he was right."

"We must have been better than we thought," Diane giggled, "That part about the pasture being all torn up means those cows were really on the move. Just like "Cow Town.""

At suppertime Aunt Polly asked, "What was the name of the movie you saw on Saturday?"

Cheryl and I shoveled potatoes into our mouths and said nothing.

Diane took a drink of milk and said, "Oh, I dunno. Something town or maybe city."

"I think I read Gene Autry's name on the billboard," Mum said, staring hard at Ross.

Without quite meeting her eyes, Ross croaked, "Did you?"

"Cow Town!" Aunt Polly said triumphantly, "I remember now. Must have been about a cattle drive. "

"If it was about a cattle drive, there probably were rustlers in the movie. Am I right, Ross?" Mum asked.

"And that's how you got the bright idea to have a cattle drive of your own, I imagine," Aunt Polly said, staring at each one of us in turn.

Ross's mouth opened and closed but no sound came out. Diane began to trace the pattern on the tablecloth with her fork. Cheryl squeezed my hand under the table. Mum and Aunt Polly exchanged glances and shook their heads.

"Out with it," Mum barked, "And we better get the whole story."

When we finished our confession, Aunt Polly thumped the table and yelled, "Kids like you are the reason mothers go gray and fathers leave home! I could cheerfully wring your necks."

To our amazement, all Mum said was, "You don't have to do the dishes tonight."

"How come?" Diane asked.

"You won't have time because you'll be busy telling Monsieur Lemay what really happened to his cows!" she shouted.

"But, he'll kill us," Ross howled.

Cheryl and I burst into tears and Diane went white.

Monsieur and Madame Lemay were sitting at their kitchen table drinking tea when we arrived.

"Entrez, entrez[10]," Madame Lemay called out, "Would you like a cup of tea?"

Mum opened the door and Aunt Polly pushed us in ahead of them.

"No thanks. The kids here have something to tell you and Monsieur Lemay," she said grimly.

Word by painful word, we told him about Gene Autry, the rustlers and our game. Monsieur Lemay listened without saying a word. Then he stood up and left the kitchen. A minute or two later, he came back with his rifle and a length of rope. He laid them carefully on the table and asked, "What happened to the rustlers in the movie?"

We stared at his rifle and the rope and swallowed hard.

"C'mon, you must remember," he insisted, "Shot were they? Or maybe hanged? After all, rustlin's a serious crime n'est-ce pas?"[11]

A heavy silence stretched uncomfortably between us and he let us squirm for what felt like an eternity. At last, he turned to his wife and asked, "What d'ya think, Lucille? Rifle, or rope or what?"

By this time, all four of us had tears running down our cheeks. Madame Lemay studied us for a minute and said to her husband, "They seem sorry for what they did. Do you think they could pay for their crime some other

---

[10] Come in, come in.

[11] Isn't it

way?"

Monsieur Lemay stroked his chin for a minute and then wagged his finger at us.

"Good idea, Lucille. Be here at 6," he said with a scowl, "All 4 of youse."

"6 o'clock?" Ross squeaked, "In the morning?"

"B'en oui,[12] and 6 o'clock tomorrow night, too."

With that Monsieur Lemay picked up his rifle and gave us one last order, "Portez vos bottes!"[13]

To say we had a restless night would be an understatement. Bleary-eyed and yawning, we presented ourselves next morning at Monsieur Lemay's stable door on the dot of 6. He handed each of us a heavy shovel and pointed at the overflowing dung channel.

"I sure don't want youse anywhere near my cows, but you can clean up after them," he growled, "Allez'y[14], and while you're shoveling, you can think about what youse did to my poor cows."

Have you any idea how hard it is, or how long it takes to clean up after a herd of cows who've been stuffing every one of their seven stomachs with grass for the past 12 hours? Can you imagine the mess, the stench and the flies? Can you imagine having to do it twice? It sure wipes the smile off your face, I can tell you that for nothing!

The notorious Stonefield Gang: One cowboy, one bank robber, two Indian chiefs, three dance hall girls and one mother and baby. (1949)

[12] Well yes

[13] Wear your boots

[14] Get going

Chapter 15

Bébé Portelance

Although I was not quite 11 years old and Bébé Portelance[15] was well past 50 the summer that he was assigned to work at Lock 5, we became good friends. Bébé was a very small man, not much taller than I was, with a bald head and flashing blue eyes. His shoes were always polished and his trousers perfectly pressed. He held himself ramrod-straight and waved his hands expressively when he talked. He told me that he'd been nicknamed Bébé by his fellow soldiers in World War I because he was only 14 when he joined up and went to France to fight for King and Country.

To show me he hadn't forgotten his training, he marched back and forth behind the lock-house one day, beating an imaginary drum and singing battle songs at the top of his lungs. Then he rolled up his shirt sleeve and showed me the scar where an enemy bullet had gone right through his arm and put

[15] Baby Portelance

him 'hors du combat'.[16]

"What did you do then?" I asked him.

Proudly he told his story, "My arm healed pretty good, but it wasn't strong enough to beat my big drum, so I was put on kitchen duty. At first I was disappointed but after a while I discovered that I loved cooking and if I do say so myself, I was very good at it."

"I'd like to learn how to cook. Would you teach me how?" I asked hopefully.

"Avec plaisir, ma chère enfant,"[17] Bébé replied enthusiastically, "I can teach you to be more than a cook. I can teach you to be a Chef, an expert in the kitchen!"

I followed him to the cookhouse and before I knew it, I was covered from chin to ankle in a snowy white apron. Bébé tied a kerchief around my neck to complete the uniform and in a voice loud enough for the parade ground ordered me to wash my hands.

I looked around curiously as I lathered the sliver of soap in the wash basin. The cookhouse fascinated me. It was a simple kitchen provided for the convenience of the men who worked at Lock 5 but because it was such a tiny building and tucked away in a grove of trees, it felt like a secret playhouse. In any case, it was a perfect place for me to learn how to cook.

Inside, there was a scaled-down wood stove, a narrow cupboard for dishes and supplies and a small table covered in red and white checked oilcloth. Two little stools were tucked under the table and a pint-sized wood-box behind the door held a few sticks of kindling and a couple of logs. Bunches of herbs dangled from the ceiling and jars of wild garlic, pickled mushrooms and cornichons[18] sparkled on the windowsill. A trap door in the floor covered a hole in the ground where Bébé kept the butter, eggs, milk and meat, nice and cool.

Over the next few weeks, Bébé showed me how to chop parsley, dice potatoes and slice carrots so thin I could see through them. Standing side by side, we sauteed onions and seared meat in an iron kettle while the temperature soared and the sweat ran down our faces. He told me stories of the war while the soup simmered and taught me the words to 'La Marseillaise' while we waited for the bread to rise.

---

[16] Out of the battle

[17] With pleasure, my dear child

[18] Gherkins

Bébé was an emotional cook. A fluffy omelet moved him to tears of joy while a souffle that fell sent him into a towering rage. A sauce that decided to separate, upset him so much that he hurled it right through the screen door onto the grass. Perfect pie crust made him so happy he danced a jig and he whooped with delight the day I surprised him with nasturtium leaves in the salad.

One glorious morning near the end of the summer, Bébé decided I was ready to tackle 'Poule en Cocotte du Midi'[19]. He rhymed off the ingredients and I lined them up on the table -- chicken, bacon, tomatoes, onions, carrots, a bouquet garni put together from the herbs overhead, salt and pepper and some olive oil, the very finest of course.

"Anything else?" I asked.

Bébé put his finger to his lips, stuck his head out the door and looked around. Then he turned to me and whispered hoarsely, "Look in the cupboard behind the bag of flour. You'll find two bottles, one large and one small. Put them on the table and cover them with a dishtowel."

I did as he asked but shot him a puzzled look.

Bébé proceeded to enlighten me, "Les français de France understand the importance of a splash of wine and a drop of brandy in fine cooking. Malheureusement[20], certain people around here would be scandalized at the very idea so we must be discreet. Comprends-tu, ma chère enfant?"[21]

I certainly did. Our minister hectored us regularly and at great length about the evils of alcohol and while some of the men in our congregation might drink a glass of beer after a hard day's work, no one in Stonefield would dare to have anything as sinful as a bottle of French wine under their roof.

I adjusted the dishtowel a little and winked conspiratorily at Bébé. We began our work and soon the little cookhouse was filled with the tantalizing aroma of chicken and vegetables browning in bacon fat and olive oil. I dropped a bouquet garni in the pot and stood back. Bébé measured out two generous cups of red wine and a small glassful of brandy. With a flourish, he poured it all into the pot, and stirred briskly for a moment or two before placing the heavy lid on top.

"Voilà," he said triumphantly, "Now we let it 'mijoter'[22] for a couple of

---

[19] Hen in a stewpot, Midi style

[20] Unfortunately

[21] Do you understand, my dear child?

[22] Simmer

hours."

We were just sitting down for a game of checkers when the telephone in the lock house shrilled. Bébé ran to answer it and rushed back to tell me that I was in charge of the 'Poule en Cocotte'.

"A boat is coming from Lock 4 so keep your two eyes on our meal. It mustn't burn! Sois sage, ma fille!"[23]

I busied myself setting the table. Then I checked the fire and gave the Poule en Cocotte a gentle stir. Through the cookhouse window I watched as a huge white yacht entered the lock. The chrome trim glittered in the sun and brightly coloured flags fluttered from the stern. Two glamorous women, dripping with jewelry and glistening with suntan oil lazed on the deck sipping tall drinks. Handsome men in jaunty caps and white trousers secured the boat with thick ropes. Bébé cranked the first set of gates closed and the lock gradually filled with water. Then he went to the next set of gates and cranked them open. He untied the ropes, threw them to the men on the yacht and signalled to them to proceed.

One of the women called out to Bébé, "Thanks for your help. Here's something special for your lunch," and she tossed a can carelessly in his direction. Bébé caught it just before it hit the ground. The yacht roared away leaving a wake of ripples and foam. Bébé held the can at arm's length and squinted at the blue and red label.

Suddenly he roared furiously, "Sacré bleu! Quelle horreur!"[24]

He shook his fist at the vanishing yacht and stomped back to the cookhouse. He thumped the can down on the table. His eyes were blazing and his hands were shaking.

"Look at that! Regardes!"[25] he commanded me.

"Cordon Bleu Meatballs and Gravy," I read aloud.

Bébé said scathingly, "Cordon Bleu, mon oeil!"[26]

"What's Cordon Bleu anyway?" I asked curiously.

Bébé said, "Cordon Bleu is food prepared by the finest of French chefs. The woman on that yacht is sadly mistaken if she believes the stuff in this can is Cordon Bleu."

"What's wrong with it?" I asked innocently.

[23] Be wise, pay attention, my girl
[24] Profanity- sacred God, what a horror
[25] Look
[26] My eye

Bébé's face went so red I thought he was going to explode.

"To start with, it's not fresh," he blustered, "And to finish, only the Bon Dieu knows what's in it! Think of our Poule en Cocotte du Midi. The chicken and bacon came from my neighbour's farm and I picked the vegetables from my own garden before I came to work this morning. Voies-tu?"[27]

"Yes, I think I do," I said excitedly, "And your wife grew the herbs herself, didn't she? And we made it all with our own hands, didn't we?"

Bébé nodded, pleased that I was beginning to understand.

"Exactement,[28]" he said with a shrug.

He turned to the stove, lifted the lid of the pot and sniffed our Poule en Cocotte du Midi. He motioned for me to do the same. As I breathed in the mouth-watering aroma, Bébé said proudly, "This, ma chère enfant, this is Cordon Bleu food. We used fresh ingredients and cooked it as well as any French chef could possibly do."

An hour later, we tucked our napkins under our chins and sat down to enjoy our 'Poule en Cocotte du Midi'. I watched anxiously as Bébé savoured his first mouthful with half-closed eyes.

"M-m-m-m," he murmured approvingly, "Delicieux[29]. You have done well, ma chère."

Thrilled by his words of praise, I picked up my fork and began to eat. The flavour was like nothing I had ever tasted before. We ate in companionable silence. Bébé mopped up the last drop of gravy from his plate with a crust of bread and leaned back with a contented sigh. We finished off our meal with a cup of milky tea for me and a pungent Gitane cigarette for Bébé. While we washed the dishes Bébé quizzed me about the recipe.

"How much bacon do you need? C'est quoi, un bouquet garni?[30] What kind of wine is best?" he wanted to know, "How long must it simmer?"

"Très bien, ma fille,[31]" he said approvingly when I answered all his questions correctly.

"Before you go, there is something of great importance I want to say to you," he said sounding unusually serious.

[27] Do you see?

[28] Exactly

[29] Delicious

[30] What is a bouquet garni?

[31] Very good, my girl

He waggled his finger under my nose, "Écoutes-moi bien.[32] When you grow up you might never be rich. You may never own a yacht. But if you cook the way I am teaching you, and if you use fresh ingredients, you will always eat like a queen and your family and friends will be honoured to come to your table. Remember that, ma Petite Chef.[33]"

I think I floated home that day. My head was full of new words and big ideas–'Poulet en Cocotte du Midi,' 'Cordon Bleu', and best of all, 'ma Petite Chef!'

Our favourite swimming spot at Lock 5
of the Grenville Canal. (1953)

[32] Listen carefully
[33] My little cook

Chapter 16

Froggie's Pool

Froggie was a sleeper. He snored through musical evenings in our church hall, sermons that threatened fire and brimstone, and the shrill nagging of his wife Ida. His neighbours nicknamed him Horiz, short for horizontal but after an encounter with him which put money in my pocket, I christened him Quick Silver.

It all began one morning when I overheard Ida complaining to Mrs. Byrne.

"What am I going to do?" she implored her friend, "Froggie stays in bed 'til gone ten, loafs on the porch 'til noon and dozes on the porch swing 'til supper. I'm sick, sore and tired of trying to get that man to do a lick of work. I'm that fed up, I could scream."

"Have a cup of tea, Ida," soothed Mrs. Byrne, "You'll manage, dear. You always have."

Ida sipped the comforting brew and her exasperation gradually evaporated like the steam from her cup. That evening, I listened along with Diane and Ross and Cheryl as Mrs. Byrne told Mum and Aunt Polly all about Ida's visit.

"Poor Ida," clucked Mrs. Byrne, "She's worn to a frazzle trying to keep that farm going all by herself. Froggie doesn't do a blessed thing."

"Well, he eats and sleeps enough for the two of them," snorted Mr. Byrne in disgust, recalling how he once tried to be of help.

" 'Now Froggie,' I said using my most persuasive voice," Mr Byrne began, " 'If you stayed awake in the forenoon you could do some chores. Then after dinner you could catch forty winks and still have time to get the cows before supper. It would be such a help to your missus.' "

"Froggie listened and even thanked me," Mr. Byrne went on, "He said, 'Well now, I appreciate your advice. I really do,' and then the old scallywag climbed into his hammock to mull it over. He's beyond help, if you ask me."

The morning after our visit to the Byrnes we got up to find it was pouring rain.

"Shucks," Diane complained, "What'll we do today? We can't play outside."

"How about helping us bake some cookies for Ida?" Mum suggested, "She could do with cheering up."

"Sure thing!" we agreed and Mum and Aunt Polly began to line up the baking things on the kitchen table.

Ross watched them from the corner of his eye and spoke meaningfully to Diane, Cheryl and me, "I bet Froggie'll sleep all day. I bet he won't even get up. After all, with this rain, I bet his barnyard will be a pool of water."

He jingled the change in his pocket and stared hard at us.

"But, I bet we could have some fun, rain or no rain," he said with a wink.

"I bet we could." Diane agreed and winked back at him.

Cheryl and I glanced at Mum. She was reading the cookie recipe and Aunt Polly was greasing the cookie sheets oblivious to the plot developing right under their noses. We got to work and soon the house was filled with the tantalizing smell of gingersnaps.

"The rain seems to be letting up so I'll trot over to Ida's after lunch," said Mum as we tidied the kitchen.

"We'll go for you," Diane offered quickly.

"Yeah," said Cheryl, "We'll spend some time with Ida to cheer her up."

"Thanks," said Mum, "How come you're so helpful all of a sudden?"

Smiling angelically we fibbed, "Just trying to be neighbourly."

We set off just after three o'clock. As soon as we rounded the corner, Ross produced a stubby pencil and a scrap of paper.

"Here's the deal. Pick the time you think Froggie'll get up, and whoever's time is closest, wins," he said.

He squinted at his watch, "Prob'ly any time after three thirty is a safe bet. I'll go first."

"No fair," Cheryl objected, "Whenever we have a pool, you always get first pick. I'm making the first bet and I want twenty to four."

Chagrined, Ross scribbled it down on the paper.

Diane jumped in next, "I'll take five to four. By then Ida'll be mad enough to pour Froggie's tea straight down his throat. I won't have to do a thing."

Ross pooh-poohed her chances, "Froggie could swallow boiling oil without waking up.

My plan's way better."

"Says who?" I asked.

"Me," he replied, "See, I know Froggie likes fishing. He can fish and sleep at the same time. I've seen him do it."

"Maybe so," sneered Diane, "but how're you gonna get him up? Smack him with a trout?"

Ross ignored her and announced, "I'm taking four oh nine."

Crossing my fingers for luck, I told him to write down four fifteen for me.

He held out his hand, "Cough up your quarters and let's go."

Ida spied us coming and dragged open her shaky door before we even knocked.

"Come in. I'm so glad to see you. I was feeling kind of lonesome," she said. I must confess that I felt a pang of guilt at what we were about to do.

"Mum and Aunt Polly sent some cookies for you," said Diane handing Ida the tin. Ida opened it and said, "Ginger snaps! My favourite. Sit down while I heat the kettle."

Froggie was stretched out on the day bed by the window snoring as loud as a pig with three snouts.

Ida bustled across the kitchen bellowing over her shoulder as she went, "Froggie! Stir your stumps. We got company."

Cheryl elbowed Ross and looked pointedly at the clock.

"Today's rain'll be good for the garden. Don't you think?" she yelled in Ida's direction, keeping an eye on Froggie at the same time.

Ida jumped and said, "Er-, um, yes, I guess so."

Froggie shifted on the narrow day bed and grunted. Cheryl began to cough. She scraped her chair back and stomped noisily over to the sink for a drink of water. She slurped it as loudly as she could. We watched Froggie but he didn't even twitch, let alone get up. Ross checked the time and crossed out Cheryl's name.

"You lose," he hissed gleefully.

Ida stirred up the fire and dropped the poker into the coal bucket with a terrible clatter.

She made the tea, slammed a tray full of crockery down on the table and screeched, "Froggie! Cuppa tea?"

Diane looked at the time, and rubbed her hands together in anticipation but Froggie didn't move a muscle. Ida banged a mug of tea down on the windowsill beside Froggie and came back to the table.

She nibbled at a cookie and asked, "Do you think your mum would give me the recipe for these cookies or is it a family secret?"

"I'm sure she'd be pleased to share it," I replied.

Ida picked up the sugar bowl and charged over to Froggie.

She dumped four spoonfuls of sugar into his mug and bawled right in his ear, "Froggie! Drink your tea! It's just how you like it, stone cold and thick as molasses."

Diane waited hopefully but Froggie didn't stir.

Ross tapped his watch and whispered, "Too bad, Diane, it's four o'clock. Froggie's still down and you're out."

Diane pouted. Ida went over to the day bed, shook Froggie's shoulder and jabbed him in the ribs half a dozen times.

"Froggie?" she hollered, her voice rising to high doh.

Ross studied his watch and said, "Oh Ida, let him sleep a bit longer. He looks so comfy."

"Doesn't he just?" Ida agreed through clenched teeth.

A minute or two later, Ross took a deep breath and launched into an ear-splitting description of a great fishing hole he'd recently discovered. Ida jumped and looked confused.

"Do you mean the creek in the sugar bush or the pond over the hill?" she quavered when he finally shut up.

Froggie yawned and clasped his hands across his big soft belly. His mouth sagged open revealing six tobacco-stained teeth.

Ross checked the time, "Never mind, Ida," he sighed, "Forget about the fishing hole. It's four eleven."

"Er, four eleven?" she echoed, looking puzzled.

Anxious to change the subject, Ida turned to us girls and asked for news from our end of Stonefield.

"Raccoons got into Mr. Owen's attic," Diane reported.

"Mrs. Beck's gone to visit her sister for a few days," Cheryl told her.

I peeked at the clock, cleared my throat loudly and piped up, "Mrs. Byrne is bottling her dandelion wine today."

Froggie shot right up. His boots scrabbled noisily on the worn linoleum.

"Did you say w-w-wine?" he jabbered rubbing the sleep from his eyes, "Mrs.

Byrne, b-b-bottling w-w-wine?"

"I sure did," I cried pleased as punch at his reaction.

Froggie galloped across the kitchen, "I'd best get over there. She'll be wanting me to sample it. Mrs. Byrne values my opinion when it comes to such matters, you know."

He positively streaked out the door and flew down the path.

"Honestly! That Froggie," Ida groaned, wringing her hands, "He's nothing but a thorn in my side."

I know I should have said something comforting to poor Ida, but instead I crowed, "Look Ross! It's four-fifteen on the dot!"

"I'll be darned!" Ross gasped, "You lucky duck."

Diane and Cheryl scowled but I smiled like the cat that got the cream.

A vision of dear Mrs. Byrne rose before my eyes. Because of her dandelion wine, I'd soon have four quarters jingling in my pocket and with any luck, I'd have a lot more by the end of the year.

You see, dear Mrs. Byrne didn't just make dandelion wine every June, she made raspberry cordial in July, elderberry wine in September and a huge sherry trifle at Christmas. Quick Silver indeed!

Horses
plodding, sweating, straining
patient, obedient,essential
harrowing the field, bringing in the hay
as noble as kings
Heroes

Candles
Waxy, smooth
Glowing, flickering, dancing
Smelling of honey
Gentle, steady
Lights

Chapter 17

Rusty and the Chickens

An invitation to have supper at Juliette and William's house was one of the high spots of our summer in the country. William had a small herd of beef cattle and an orchard with four different kinds of apples. Juliette kept a large flock of chickens, depending on their eggs for her baking and their meat for delectable stews, soups and pies. As well, they had a large herb garden and an enormous strawberry patch. Needless to say the meals that came out of Juliettte's kitchen were always delicious.

So, filled with anticipation we set off one peaceful summer afternoon to join Juliette and William for supper. Our mouths watered as we talked about all the lovely possibilities in store for us. Cheryl had her heart set on a jellied salad decorated with cucumber slices. Ross and Diane were hoping for succulent roast chicken with sage and onion dressing. Uncle Len waxed eloquent about crepes filled with apples and whipped cream and I rhapsodized over Juliette's angel cake. Dad said a good thick slice of roast beef wouldn't go amiss while Mum said she was sure whatever Juliette served would be wonderful and we kids were to mind our manners and clean our plates.

As we strolled and chatted, our dog, Rusty scampered off to follow inter-esting scents and then raced back to catch up with us. Aunt Polly was carrying Rusty's leash because Juliette was adamant that no dog, not even our beloved Rusty, should ever cross her doorstep.

"Le bon Dieu gave us animals for the stable and the table, not for the parlour," she said firmly the very first time we visited. So, like it or not, Rusty had to stay outside tethered to the gate post.

We rounded the last bend in the road. Before us lay an idyllic pastoral scene. Juliette and William's pretty yellow house snuggled up against a steep hill. Huge maple trees marked the end of their long curving driveway, making a leafy frame for the front yard. Juliette's flock of fat speckled leghorns dotted the wide lawn.

Aunt Polly called to Rusty, "Sorry old fella, but it's time to put on your leash."

Rusty took one look at the leash and ran away as fast as his legs could carry him. Mum groaned with exasperation, "Holy smoke! Better go after him, kids."

Rusty had a considerable lead and his curly tail bobbed along a good hundred feet in front of us. We started running.

"Good dog, here boy, here boy," Diane called. Rusty's easy trot became a gallop.

Uncle Len shouted at us, "Hurry up, there's going to be trouble if he gets into Juliette's house."

We doubled our speed and Dad joined in the chase.

"Heel, you wretched animal," he bellowed. Rusty bolted up the driveway and headed straight for the hens. He was delighted to find fel-low creatures to play with. Yapping deliriously he nipped at their feath-ered bottoms. The indignant hens squawked and flapped their wings. Ju-liette bounded out of her rocking chair on the porch and flew down the steps. William came round the corner of the house puffing on his pipe. "What's going on?" he asked.

Juliette chased after Rusty, screeching, "Méchant chien, arrêtes, ar-rêtes.[34]"

Rusty ignored her. He zigzagged his way through the flock barking excit-edly. The hens cackled and pecked at him. Desperate to escape, they fled every

---

[34] Wicked dog. Stop, stop.

which way. Rusty was having a whale of a time. His eyes were half-closed and his tongue lolled out of his mouth. Uncle Len covered the last few feet of the driveway, his long legs churning like pistons. When he came face to face with the chaotic scene, his eyes bugged out with shock.

Juliette yelled frantically, "Do something, Len."

"Come back at once you miserable mutt," he roared in a voice loud enough to stop an army in its tracks and took off after the dog.

Juliette followed Uncle Len, waving her plump arms and shouting, "Mon Dieu, mon Dieu! Catch that darn dog, Len, before he kills my hens."

William yelled at us, "C'mon, kids. Spread out. We'll try and trap him."

"Head him off at the woodshed," Dad shouted. I sprinted as fast as I could but Rusty scampered easily out of my reach. Ross dashed by grinning madly and waving a broom around like King Arthur's sword.

"Cease and desist, you wretched varmint," he roared, "Or I shall impale you."

Cheryl pulled a large towel from the clothesline and tried to throw it over Rusty's head. My sides ached from laughing and Diane had tears running down her cheeks.

"This is just like a Ma and Pa Kettle movie," she gasped.

Dad charged back and forth, bawling orders at us and shouting threats at Rusty. Mum stood stock-still on the sidelines, holding her head in her hands. Juliette chased after Uncle Len, wringing her hands and calling on all the saints of heaven to intervene.

Aunt Polly, on the other hand, was enjoying the chaos. Never one to take life too seriously, she joined in the race and called gaily to Juliette, "Stop chasing my husband, you shameless hussy."

She smoothed back her hair and called, "It took me six years to catch him. You haven't got a chance."

Turning on her, Juliette cried angrily, "Chasing your husband? Chasing your husband?"

Her face went purple and she sputtered, "I'm trying to save my hens. It's not a joke. I need them to feed my family next winter."

"Oh Juliette," Aunt Polly stammered, "I'm so sorry."

That's when I realized that this wasn't anything like a Ma and Pa Kettle movie after all.

Our dog was literally taking the food off Juliette and William's table.

"He's heading your way," Dad shouted, "Now's your chance."

Before we could react, Rusty suddenly flopped down on the grass to catch his breath. Dad grabbed him by the scruff of his neck and shook him angrily. He insulted his ancestry, his intelligence, and his lack of moral fiber.

William said quietly, "Don't let him go, whatever you do. I'll look around to see how many of the hens are still alive."

"I'll give you a hand," said Uncle Len.

Mum snapped Rusty's leash onto his collar without saying a word.

The rest of us stood around in embarrassed silence, unable to look Juliette in the eye. Feathers floated gently on the breeze and skinny chicken feet stuck out from some very odd places. We could hear feeble squawks and weak gasping noises. The men came back looking grim. Uncle Len cleared his throat and Dad fanned his face with his hat.

"Juliette, my dear," William said sadly, "I'm sorry to tell you that only about six hens have survived."

Appalled, we waited for Juliette's reaction to this dreadful news. Using the hem of her apron to mop the perspiration from her face, she shook her head in despair. She didn't say a word.

Dad apologized, "Juliette, I'm so sorry. What can I say? Rusty's used to chasing pigeons in the city and I guess he thought it was the same thing when he saw your hens."

Aunt Polly put her arm around Juliette's shoulders and said soberly, "I'm sorry I joked about you running after Len. I shouldn't have said that."

Mum spoke up, "We'll come to an arrangement about the damage Rusty caused and I promise we won't bring him with us the next time."

"If there ever is a next time," Uncle Len muttered.

"In the meantime," Aunt Polly suggested quietly, "I think it would be best if we left."

Sadly we murmured our good-byes. Rusty trotted obediently at Diane's heels all the way home and slunk off to his basket as soon as Dad opened our front door. Mum and Aunt Polly dished up beans on toast for supper.

We bowed our heads while Cheryl prayed, "For what we are about to receive may the Lord make us truly thankful," but if anybody said amen, I sure didn't hear it.

Rusty, before he disgraced himself. (1948)

Soft as cobwebs
The mist enfolds me
I close my eyes and pray
At peace

Kindling
Light-weight, flimsy
Slivered, broken, chipped
Starting the fire
Starting the day
Important

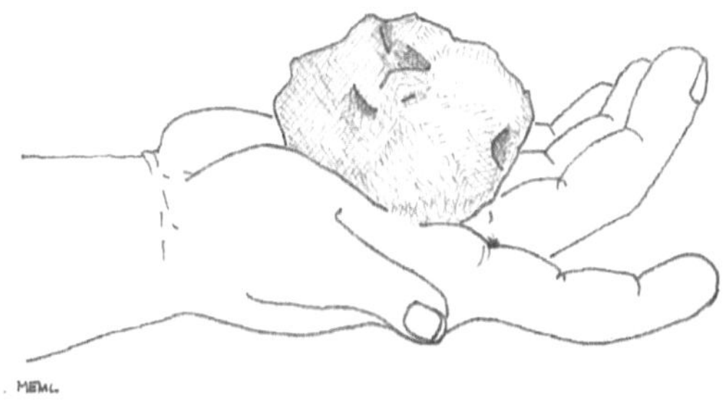

Chapter 18

Stones

One day my friend Henny and I were playing in the creek, piling up stones and rocks to make waterfalls and dams. Henny and her family had recently emigrated from Holland and lived nearby in a farmhouse between Lock 4 and Lock 5. While we played,we chatted about everything and nothing.I remember that the sun filtering through the leaves of the butternut tree dappled the water with dazzling silver glints. I recall how pleasant it was to feel the cool water swirling around my ankles.

"Do you like living here better than Holland?" I asked her.

"Oh yes, things are much better for us in Canada," she replied quickly.

We dragged a large flat rock into the center of the creek and watched with satisfaction as the water curled and eddied around it.

"What's better?" I asked curiously.

"Well, we have a lot more to eat and people here are nice to us. Our neighbours invite us to their houses and when we go to town, everyone says hello. Even people who don't know us," she said with a smile.

Henny lugged a heavy rock from the bank of the creek. We wedged it underneath our big flat stone and blocked the water on each side with a few smaller stones. The water tumbled over the stones and splashed our legs.

"That worked really well," I said, "Let's build something else."

Henny nodded, "Sure, this is fun."

We picked our way upstream and gathered stones of all shapes and sizes. We piled them up on the bank of the creek and stood back to admire our fine collection.

"Don't you love stones?" I asked Henny, running my hands over one especially smooth one.

"I like Canadian stones," said Henny tossing a pebble from one hand to the other, "But not Dutch ones."

"Why is that?" I asked curiously.

Henny tugged a large stone out of the pile we had made and dragged it to the middle of the creek. I took several smaller ones and handed them to her one by one. She wedged them firmly around the base of the big stone and stood back to study the result before answering my question.

"In Holland, people sometimes threw big stones at our house and broke the windows," she said, watching the water through narrowed eyes, "And I remember a few times when we were walking on the street they threw small stones at us."

"They did?" I asked, shocked, "But why?"

"Because we're different. We're Jews," she said matter-of-factly.

She was looking around for more stones but I stood stock-still and stared at her.

"Jews?" I repeated, "What are Jews?"

"People like me and my family," Henny said.

Puzzled, I blinked at Henny, "But Henny, your family looks like my family. You have brown hair and blue eyes and so do I. Your dad and mine both have black hair and our mums both have brown eyes. Does that mean if my family went to Holland, people would throw stones at us?"

"Henny shrugged, "I dunno. They didn't throw stones at everybody, just some of us."

"Well, I don't get it," I said.

We stood silently in the middle of the creek just looking at each other. Suddenly Henny shivered and stepped out of the water onto the grass.

"I don't feel like playing any more. I'm going home," she said and she turned and left.

"See you tomorrow?" I called after her.

"Maybe," she called back over her shoulder.

Henny and I didn't play in the creek again that summer. Somehow the sun was never warm enough and the water was always too cold. As for the stones—I don't know about Henny but I couldn't bear to touch them any more.

The creek
trickling and gurgling
cooling my feet, soothing my soul
A rill

Rain
Soft, gentle
Falling, dripping, drumming
Water, mist, diamonds, beads
Pleasing, cleansing, quenching
Undeserved, welcome
A blessing

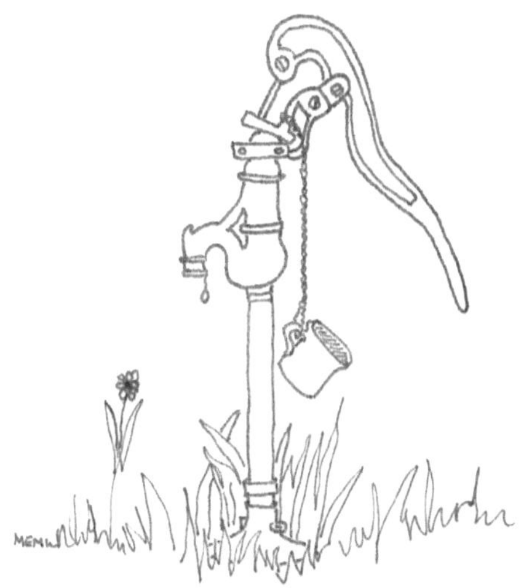

Chapter 19

Cold Water

Mum and Aunt Polly liked nothing better than the challenge of a new berry patch, so when they heard that Mr. Dawson's wood-lot was full of raspberries we knew we were about to be corralled into a couple of hours of serious picking.

"Mrs. Dawson doesn't make raspberry jam any more. She said the seeds get under her new plates[35] and hurt like the dickens. She told us we could help ourselves," Aunt Polly said happily.

Ross listened, then said doubtfully, "But isn't their wood-lot near the Stonefield Station? That's a heck of a long way to go for a few berries."

"Nonsense," Mum scoffed, "It's not even a mile away."

Aunt Polly passed out the berry pails.

"The sooner we get going, the sooner we'll get back," she said briskly.

---

[35] Dentures

Mum and Aunt Polly walked ahead of us talking nonstop about how many jars of jam they would be making. The sun was unmercifully hot and we kids stopped to rest every time we came to a shady spot. Of course, Mum and Aunt Polly reached the berry patch before us and seemed surprised that we weren't right on their heels.

"Hurry up," Mum called, "Choose a spot and pick all the berries within reach before you move on."

Even though the berries were so ripe they just about fell into our pails by themselves, it wasn't an easy job. In no time, sweat was rolling down our backs. Insects niggled and buzzed around our ears, adding to our misery. Robins called over and over for rain and tree toads kept up their piercing cry warning of more heat to come.

Bumblebees staggered from buttercup to corn-flower stupefied by the heavy warm air and dazzled by the sun.

"I'm suffocating," I wailed before my pail was even half full.

"I'm being bitten to death," Ross called out slapping his neck crossly.

"A snake just slithered across my foot," Diane screeched.

Cheryl whined, "I think I just touched some poison ivy. I'm itchy already."

"Heavens above," Mum snapped, "What a bunch of complainers. You're happy enough to spread the jam on your toast every morning, so dry up and keep picking."

After what felt like hours, Aunt Polly sang out, "Let's see your pails. They should be full by now."

Dutifully we held them out for her inspection.

"Not bad at all," Aunt Polly pronounced.

"Better than I expected," Mum agreed.

"Does that mean we can go home?" Diane asked, fanning her face with her hat.

"It does," Mum replied.

"I can't walk all the way home unless I get a drink, "Ross said flatly, "I'm parched and that's worse than thirsty."

Mum mopped her forehead and said, "We're all hot and thirsty, but there's no water around here so…."

"Look," Diane said, pointing to a chimney poking up above a hedge a short distance away, "There's a house. We can ask for a drink of water there."

"Don't be silly," Ross snorted, "That's the Sloan farm. No one goes there, remember?"

"Really? That's the Sloan place?" Diane gasped, "People say the two sisters who live there are actually witches."

"What a load of codswallop," Mum said, "They're just two poor old souls trying to scratch a living out of their farm."

"And you should know better than to listen to gossip," Aunt Polly added, "I say we go over and ask them for a drink. Who knows? Maybe they'll actually be glad to see us."

We trailed up the road to the farm and stood stock-still at their gate, staring at the scene before us. Bits of farm equipment lay willy-nilly around the yard. The manure pile was higher than the mossy roof of the stable and the house was so crooked, it looked as though it might come apart at the seams at any minute. Silently Cheryl pointed to a rusty pump half-hidden in the tall grass.

"Water," she whispered, "If it still works."

Mum pushed the gate open and said, "I'm sure the Misses Sloan won't mind if we use it but I'll go and ask anyway."

She picked her way across the unkempt yard and stepped up onto the porch. We followed at a safe distance and waited in a little knot at the foot of the stairs.

Mum rapped on the door and called out, "Yoo-hoo. Is anybody home? It's Mrs. Harkness from Stonefield."

No reply. Aunt Polly cupped her hands around her mouth and shouted, "We'd like a drink of water."

The door creaked open just enough for one beady eye to peer out at us. Four gnarled fingers curled around the edge of the door.

"Good morning, Miss –er-er-Sloan," Mum stammered, "Could we trouble you for some water? The children are thir---"

"Pump's over there," the woman croaked. She shut the door with a thud, leaving Mum standing there blinking at the flaking green paint.

"Could we have a cup, please?" Mum called.

A few seconds elapsed before the door inched open and the eye peered out again.

"On the pump."

The face disappeared. Gingerly we picked our way to the pump. The enamel dipper was badly chipped and pocked with rust. Heaven only knows how long it had been hanging there. Mum and Aunt Polly made signs to us not to touch it and we didn't. Diane pumped furiously and after a series of groans and shrieks, beautiful clear, cold water gushed into our cupped hands. We gulped it down thankfully and splashed some on our hot faces.

"Hurry up and let's get out of here. This place gives me the willies," Aunt

Polly whispered to us.

"Thanks for the water," we called in the direction of the house. Our words floated eerily across the silence.

"Do you think they're watching us?" Diane asked.

She took a few steps towards the house, staring intently at the kitchen window where a grubby curtain twitched every once in a while. She didn't notice Ross stealthily edging up behind her.

"Boo!" he shouted, giving her a sharp poke in the back.

Diane screamed and we all jumped. She spun around and grabbed Ross by his shirt.

"You think you're so funny, well, let's see how funny you think this is," she yelled.

She yanked him by the arm with such force that he lost his balance. Pressing her advantage, Diane dragged him onto the porch and shoved him up against the weather-beaten wall of the house with a loud thump. His shoes made a scrabbling sound on the bare boards as he tried to get away. He and Diane wrestled and rolled off the porch, landing on the grass in a tangle of flailing arms and legs.

"Stop it this instant, or else," shouted Mum crossly.

Cheryl and I watched in alarm as the door inched open again. Our mothers gasped when, instead of the craggy face they expected to see, the business end of a shotgun appeared.

"Get down, get down," Aunt Polly screamed.

We dived into the long grass and held our breath.

"Pow!" A shot cracked over our heads, nearly deafening us. The sound rolled across the open fields and echoed back from the hills.

Mum sprang up from her hiding-place and shouted furiously, "What do you think you're doing? You should be ashamed of yourself, firing that thing at innocent women and children."

But she was talking to herself. The shotgun had vanished and the door was shut tight. We got to our feet and made our way to the road on shaking legs. Mum and Aunt Polly hustled us away down the road at breakneck speed. Our pails bumped against our legs. Raspberries bounced out and rolled away unnoticed.

When we reached the safety of our house, we sat around the dining-room table drinking lemonade and talking about our lucky escape. After a while, we kids left Mum and Aunt Polly smoking cigarettes to calm their nerves and trying to decide whether to lodge a complaint with the mayor, the police, the doctor, or all three.

We climbed to our usual perches in the apple tree and in no time, Ross, Diane and Cheryl were giggling and making light of what had happened that morning.

"I wasn't really scared of that old woman," Diane boasted.

"Me neither. I bet she couldn't hit the side of a barn," Ross scoffed.

"Might be fun to act it all out," Cheryl said dreamily, "I think I'd be great as Miss Sloan," and she mussed up her hair, pulled a branch down to hide one side of her face and leered at me, cackling like a witch. She scared the liver and lights out of me but Diane and Ross laughed their heads off.

"It sure would make a great play," Diane said, "Let's do it."

They started chattering about costumes and props and in no time they were arguing fiercely about who would play the lead.

"I'm the tallest, and that old hag was tall, so I should have the lead," Cheryl insisted.

Diane declared she wasn't afraid of guns so the lead should be hers.

"I wouldn't miss when I fired, either," she bragged.

Ross tried to convince them that he could look scarier and sound meaner than they could, so he should be Miss Sloan. I didn't say a word but I decided then and there that if I had to be in their silly play, I'd be the other Miss Sloan--- the one we never saw.

The apple tree
Gnarled with age
Invites us to climb into her arms
We whisper, we dream, we rest
Our cradle

Plum tree
Graceful, bent
Budding, flowering, blooming
Offering us fruit
As familiar as home
Old friend

Chapter 20

Roast Pork and Ructions

We Presbyterians grumbled about our minister because he was never satisfied with our weekly givings. Our Irish Catholic neighbours complained about their priest because his sermons were too long. But compared to our French Catholic friends down the river, we had it easy.

Their 'Monsieur le Curé' lectured them about mortal sin, venial sin and every other kind of sin until they were fed up to the back teeth listening to him. He was so bad-tempered that the old people prayed fervently not to die in Holy Week for fear of annoying him at such a busy time in the church calendar.

He agreed nicely enough to baptise new babies, but he had his own ideas about suitable names. On more than one occasion, he handed a baby back to its flabbergasted parents with a name they hadn't considered at all. But he saved his worst rants to warn his flock about the dangers of mingling with us Protestants.

"Les Protestants," he informed them, "have hearts that are black. They are unbelievers who will cause you to sin. Stay away from them."

Most of his congregation took his warnings with a big grain of salt. After all, there was only one bar in Stonefield and the men, Catholic and Protestant, quite enjoyed chewing the fat over a glass or two of beer on Saturday night. Most of the women got together for quilting parties, minded each other's children if need be and regularly dropped in on each other for a cup of tea and a chat. They were friends and neighbours, but they were discreet, all the same.

Two of his parishioners, Thérèse and André, were very good friends with our Mum and Dad. They were devout Catholics, attending mass every Sunday morning and reciting the rosary every night, and while they were as careful as anybody else not to get Monsieur le Curé riled up, they often came to our house and invited us to theirs.

Mum worried in case Monsieur le Curé got wind of these visits, but Dad scoffed and said "You're worrying for nothing. Besides can you think of anyone around here who would go running to the priest to tattle about a little thing like Thérèse and André having a meal or a game of cards with us?"

I'll never forget the day that he got the answer to that question. Thérèse and André had invited Mum, Dad, my sister Diane and I to come for supper on Friday night. We were looking forward to it because every meal we had at their house seemed to be better than the one before.

André grew wonderful vegetables and berries and he raised prize pigs. His doe-eyed Jersey cow produced a steady stream of rich milk and his beehives practically overflowed with honey. Thérèse was an outstanding cook. Potatoes were mashed with butter and cream to smooth perfection. Her meat swam in pools of rich brown gravy. Her piecrust broke into a shower of golden flakes at the touch of a fork and her meringue melted like snowflakes on the tongue.

The day in question was very warm so Thérèse had set the table in the screened porch that stretched across the front of their house.

"It'll be cooler out here," Thérèse said, "I love cooking on my wood stove, but it makes the house very hot," and she fanned her face with her apron.

"Sit down, sit down, make yourselves at home," André said hospitably. The smell coming from the kitchen was divine. Thérèse bustled to the table bearing a succulent leg of pork studded with garlic. Crispy roasted potatoes and glazed onions circled the meat and sprigs of rosemary added a fragrant touch. Two tantalizing vegetable dishes came next followed by an enormous jug of golden brown gravy.

André sharpened the carving knife and sliced the meat. With a wink at my sister and me he dropped a piece of crackling onto our plates and a generous slice of pork as well. The vegetables were handed round and last but not least we helped ourselves to the gravy.

"B'en, my gosh, I nearly forgot the applesauce," Thérèse said and she dashed away to get it.

Satisfied that the meal was now complete, she sat down, picked up her fork and said, "Bon appetit, mes amies."[36]

"Bon appetit," we chorused and picked up our forks.

Everything was cooked to perfection and we settled down to enjoy ourselves. Dad and André talked about baseball and the possibility of an election in the fall, while Mum and Thérèse talked about recipes and the number of darts needed to make a dress fit really well.

A comfortable lull in the conversation was shattered when Thérèse suddenly leapt to her feet and shrieked, "Mon Dieu, I don't believe it!"

She pointed at a car that was inching its way down the lane that led to their house. André peered through the screen and his face reddened with dismay. "Calvaire,[37]" he growled, "It's my cousin Jean-Jacques with Cécile, that nosy God-bothering wife of his. That's all we need."

Diane and I gaped in astonishment as Thérèse snatched the platter of roast pork off the table and ran into the kitchen, calling back over her shoulder, "Quick! Quick! Bring your plates and anything else you can carry."

André jumped up and said, "I'll keep them outside as long as I can."

Dad asked, "Whatever's the matter, André?"

"B'en c'est vendredi,[38] it's Friday," André said with a shrug, "And Cécile is more Catholic than the Pope."

Diane and I looked blankly at each other and turned to Mum for enlightenment.

She leaned across the table and whispered, "It's a sin for Catholics to eat meat on Friday. If Cécile tells the priest about this meal, he'll give Thérèse and André what for, so help get this table cleared."

André ran down the steps and greeted the visitors with false heartiness. We heard him insisting that they take a look at his garden. As he steered them past the porch he was talking loudly about green beans, carrots and tomato plants. André seemed interested but Cécile clearly wasn't listening. She kept looking back towards the porch with a puzzled frown on her face. At one

---

[36] Good appetite, my friends
[37] Calvary (a swear word in French)
[38] Well, it's Friday

point she stopped, lifted her nose in the air and sniffed like a mouse looking for cheese.

"Cécile, come and see André's garden," her husband called and thank goodness, she went.

In the kitchen Thérèse clapped her hand to her forehead and wailed, "If Cécile finds out that we were eating meat she'll be hammering on Monsieur le Curé's door to tell him about it before the day is out and we'll be on our knees for the rest of our natural lives."

She threw a pile of clean cutlery onto a tray and told Diane and me to lay the table with two more places.

She dumped a stack of plates down with a clatter and said, "Put these around but keep watching and warn me when Cécile heads back to the house."

We skipped around the table as fast as we could and glanced out at the yard every couple of seconds.

We heard the sound of breaking glass and Thérèse cried, "Never mind, never mind, just kick the pieces under the table."

Diane and I took our eyes off the yard for a minute to take a peek into the kitchen. The place was a shambles. Thérèse was dashing around the kitchen slamming cupboard doors, rummaging in drawers and scrabbling through cans and jars in the pantry. Dad was hacking at a big loaf of crusty bread at one end of the table, while Mum was trying to chop shallots and slice tomatoes at the other. We heard Thérèse begging all the saints of heaven to strike Cécile down in her tracks and make her blind, deaf and dumb for good measure.

She paused every so often to flap a dishtowel wildly over her head in a futile attempt to get rid of the smell of roast pork. Shocked at such chaos, Diane and I crept back to our post. Jean-Jacques and André were sauntering towards the house, but Cécile was trotting ahead of them with a very determined look in her eye.

"She's coming, she's coming," we yelled.

Thérèse mopped the perspiration off her face with her apron and shot down the steps to greet her guests.

She kissed Cécile on both cheeks, gave Jean-Jacques gave a hug and turned to introduce us, "Cécile, Jean-Jacques, I'd like you to meet our friends, Bill and Dorothy, and their daughters, Diane and Sheila."

Cécile nodded curtly and pushed past us into the porch. She sniffed loudly two or three times. The unmistakable smell of roast pork and garlic hung in the air like a line of wet washing. Her eyes raked over the table and seeing nothing untoward, she frowned. Jean-Jacques seemed oblivious both to the smell and the peculiar behaviour of his wife.

114

Turning to Mum and Dad, he said politely, "André's told me a bit about you. City folks aren't you?"

By now Cécile was craning her neck to see into the kitchen. Her nostrils were flared and she had a look of deep concentration on her face. She was taking very deep breaths.

Dad explained that we did live in the city most of the year but spent our summers in the country.

Cécile gave Mum a piercing look.

"You spend all summer here?" she asked suspiciously.

"Yes, we do," Mum admitted.

"I've never seen you in church," Cécile snapped.

Mum cleared her throat and swallowed hard.

"Well, actually we go to the Presbyterian church," she croaked.

Cécile sucked in her breath and closed her eyes. Diane and I stared at her. Her lips tightened and she fingered the crucifix at her neck.

Mon Dieu, les Protestants!"[39] she whispered faintly and crossed herself.

"We were just about to have some supper," André said loudly, "and I see Thérèse has already set places for you so sit down and we'll eat."

"I'll help you, Thérese," said Mum and they disappeared into the kitchen.

The meat platter came back but this time it held a pile of lettuce leaves and a hastily arranged salmon salad. Some raggedly sliced tomatoes and a handful of pickles were thrown on top. The bread, some of it as thick as doorsteps and the rest as thin as paper, was squashed into a basket. The gravy jug was now filled with what looked like lemonade although there wasn't a lemon slice or a mint leaf to be seen. A hunk of cheese, plunked lopsidedly on a saucer, completed the meal.

Thérèse looked at her guests and blushed with embarrassment. She said, "I apologize for the -er,-um informal meal. It was just too hot to cook today."

Mum and Dad did their best to look enthusiastic and complimented Thérèse.

"Such a treat to have salmon," Mum said brightly.

Dad said, "Nothing better than lettuce and tomatoes on a hot day, don't you think?"

No one answered. Cécile picked at her food, sniffed several times and then smiled ingratiatingly at Thérèse.

"A person might think you had been cooking all day, it's so hot in here," she said slyly.

---

[39] My God, Protestants

She sniffed again and watched Thérèse through narrowed eyes. Thérèse took a long drink of her lemonade and said nothing.

"You might think I'm 'complètement folle'[40]," Cécile continued, "but as soon as I stepped out of the car, I thought I could smell roast pork. More than that," she tittered, keeping an eye on Thérèse, "I could even smell garlic but there's no garlic in this salad as far as I can tell. Isn't that strange?"

"M-m-m, very strange. Would you like a slice of bread? It was fresh from the baker today," Thérèse replied, holding out the basket.

Cécile scowled and reluctantly picked up a piece with her thumb and forefinger.

"Of course, I know that you would never serve pork on a Friday," she said pointedly, "particularly since Monsieur le Curé reminded us only last Sunday that we are duty-bound as good Catholics to eat fish on Friday."

Thérèse and André did not rise to the bait. Dad kept his eyes glued to his plate while Mum sent warning looks at Diane and I to stay quiet, and we did. Jean-Jacques cleared his throat and looked directly at his wife.

"Monsieur le Curé says a lot of things," he said tartly, "It doesn't do to take him too seriously. I don't!"

Cécile cast a furious look at her husband. Thérèse and André realised they had an ally and smiled with relief. Mum and Dad started to chatter about the trouble they had with skunks living under the shed. André and Jean-Jacques responded with advice about how to get rid of the pests, and Thérèse told a funny story about coming face to face with a skunk in the henhouse.

Cécile didn't say a word.

Diane and I helped clear the table for dessert. Mum placed the teapot at the end of the table and covered it with a tea-cozy to keep it hot. With a triumphant flourish, Thérèse placed a gorgeous strawberry shortcake in the center of the table.

"Voilà!"[41] she said, "The strawberries are from André's garden and I churned the cream this morning.

Dad cried, "Strawberry short-cake, my favourite!"

"Mine, too," Mum echoed with delight.

"Nothing more delicious than strawberry short-cake, I always say," Jean-Jacques added.

Cécile said nothing. Mum poured out the tea. It was steaming—just like you-know-who!

---

[40] Completely mad
[41] There

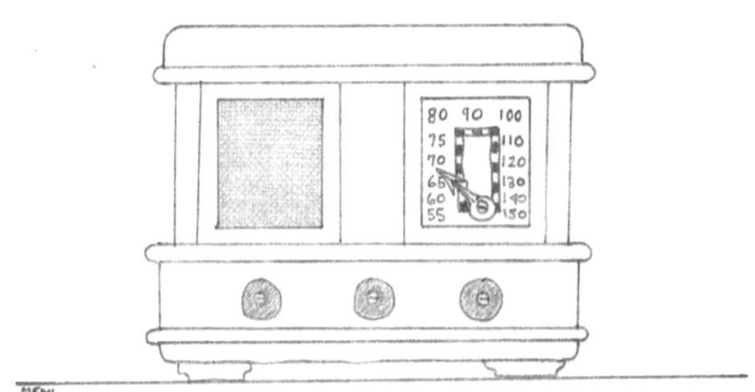

Chapter 21

Rock Around the Clock

The number one song on the 'Hit Parade' in the summer of 1955 was 'Rock Around the Clock' by Bill Haley and the Comets. Diane, Ross, Cheryl and I all thought it was the absolute living end. Every day after lunch, we tuned into radio station CFRA in Ottawa to listen to the most popular songs of the day.

The format was always the same. The deejay started with number 20 and played every song down to number 1. We danced and sang at the top of our lungs and were just about worn out by the time he yelled into the mike that the one, the only, the number one song of the day was about to be played.

Mum and Aunt Polly didn't mind us dancing and they put up with our racket but they usually tried to get us to do some chores at the same time.

Sometimes they called out over the music, "Flick a duster over the tables while you're at it," or "Push the dust mop around a couple of times, why don't you?"

We sighed heavily and rolled our eyes but in the end we did as they asked and they were happy, except of course for that unfortunate day they said, "Squeeze the margarine."

Mum and Aunt Polly were on an economy drive that summer so they were buying margarine instead of butter. It came in an attractive yellow carton, and pictured a dimpled girl decked out in an old-fashioned blue bonnet. Inside the box was a disgusting lump of hard white fat sealed in a thick plastic bag. There was a capsule of yellow food colouring inside that looked like a malevolent eye or a lost belly-button.

In order to make this stuff look like butter we had to squeeze the sac until the fat softened. Then we had to burst the bubble and keep kneading the whole sorry mess until it was uniformly yellow.

Anyway, on the day in question, Diane started the process because she had the strongest hands. We turned the radio up as loud as we dared and began to dance.

We swayed to 'Sincerely 'and stomped across the floor and back to 'Sixteen Tons'.

Diane threw the margarine to Cheryl. She held it close to warm it up and waltzed dreamily all the way through 'Only You 'and 'Unchained Melody'. I took over the bag and jived and kneaded my way through 'Dance With Me, Henry'. This last song was one of our favorites and we shouted out the lyrics and jumped around like hens on hot bricks. By now the margarine was so soft it was almost liquid.

Ross inherited the bag and he waved it high above his head as the announcer's voice rose to an ear-splitting scream, "And now, here it is, the number one song of the day, the one you've been waiting for, the one that's been at the top of the charts for weeks, the one, the only, 'Rock Around the Clock' with Bill Haley and the Comets!"

Ross pinched the capsule of dye with all his might and the bilious colour streaked through the fat. We threw the limp bag back and forth and danced energetically to the thumping beat.

"Rock"(squeeze) "around"(squeeze)"the clock"(squeeze) "to-night", we bellowed along with Bill Haley, building up to the great crescendo that we knew signaled the end of the song. In a positive frenzy of Rock and Roll ecstasy, Ross flung the margarine on the floor.

The bag burst and the revolting mess oozed out all over the linoleum. It meandered lazily across the floor to the dining room where it eddied in a yellow pool around the stone door stop. For a few seconds, we were too shocked to speak.

Then we began to laugh.

"Did you hear the smack when it hit the floor?" hiccoughed Diane.

"Did you see Ross' face when the bag split?" Cheryl cackled.

"Rock around the mess," I screeched.

"One o'clock, two o'clock, three o'clock, Oops!" roared Ross.

We stopped laughing pretty sharpish when Mum and Aunt Polly came to investigate and cleaning up the greasy puddle was very sobering, but fifty-some years later, we still laugh like the carefree teen-agers we were as soon as any one of us chants, "Rock (pause) around (pause) the clock tonight!"

Fields
Rippling, waving, welcoming
Green, gold, copper
Grain for our bread, feed for the horses
As precious as life itself
Pastures

Flames
Blazing hot
Snapping, leaping, crackling
As lively as crickets
Fire

Chapter 22

Uncle Dick

Labour Day weekend was a time of mixed emotions for Diane and me. It signaled the end of our summer in Stonefield which made us very sad, and heralded the yearly visit of our Uncle Dick, which filled us with excitement.

Uncle Dick was Mum's half-brother and although he was almost 20 years older than she was, they were very close. They were both small people, Mum being just a little under five feet tall and Uncle Dick a speck over. They had the same soft brown eyes and thick wavy hair and the same quick smile. Uncle Dick had a bushy moustache which tickled when he kissed us and he always presented Diane and me with a box of Laura Secord candy as soon as he got off the train.

Uncle Dick was an early riser and we could hear him humming to himself as he performed his 'daily dozen' as he called his morning exercises before coming down for breakfast. He arrived at the table, impeccably dressed in a three-piece tweed suit, his hair carefully brushed and combed and his shoes polished to a dazzling shine.

Uncle Dick relished his food so Diane and I had to wait patiently while he put two eggs, four rashers of bacon and two slices of toast and jam 'behind his tie' as he said. We were hopping from one foot to the other by the time he emptied the teapot, desperate to get him outside to show him all our favourite haunts. Even that turned out to be a slow process because wherever we went, the neighbours spotted him and scurried out of their houses to speak to him.

These conversations all went something like this:

Neighbour: "Well, now. You're a sight for sore eyes. How are you?"

Uncle Dick: "Good morning. Nice to see you again. I'm fine, thanks. And yourself?"

Neighbour: "Oh, can't complain. Well, I could, but who'd listen? Hope you brought your violin with you."

Uncle Dick: "I did, I did. Wouldn't dream of coming to Stonefield without it."

Neighbour: "That's grand then. We'll see you tonight then, right?"

Uncle Dick: "You can depend on it."

When Diane and I finally got him to ourselves, we steered him along the canal road to admire the By-wash and then led him through the woods to the river so he could listen to the exciting roar and clatter of the rapids and watch the fish jump.

Uncle Dick was a fount of knowledge about the birds that sang overhead and the trees and wildflowers that grew around us. Best of all, unlike most adults, he seemed to have all the time in the world to explain things to us. No question was too trivial for him to answer and no remark was brushed aside. Having his undivided attention made us feel extra special.

But the highlight of every Labour Day weekend was without a doubt, Saturday evening. And not just for our family, but for everyone in Stonefield. Starting around seven o'clock the neighbours started gathering at the Byrnes' place. Mr. Byrne set chairs all around the store to accommodate the adults and placed cushions and low stools in the middle of the room for the small children. Seeing as this was a special occasion the bigger boys and girls were allowed to sit on the counters.

The ladies arrived wearing pretty dresses, the men in white shirts and newly pressed trousers while the kids had on their Sunday best. Each family brought a shoebox filled with food to share later on.

When we arrived with Uncle Dick and his violin, everyone crowded around to greet him. We stood back and watched proudly as he shook hands, kissed cheeks and called everyone by name. At last we took our places. The chattering stopped. Uncle Dick opened his violin case and carefully rubbed the bow with rosin.

Then with a wink at us kids, he put a snow-white handkerchief on his shoulder, tucked his violin under his chin and played a saucy little jig. Everyone clapped when it was over and people began to call out requests for their favourite songs. Uncle Dick played them all and more besides. Of course he didn't ignore the children and got us all singing along and doing the actions to 'Pop! Goes the Weasel', 'Underneath the Old Umbrella' and 'Who Killed Cock Robin?'

He brought a tear to many an eye when he played and sang the haunting, 'My Ain Folk' and 'I'll Take You Home Again, Kathleen'. Then he had us all laughing when he sang, "There was I, Waitin' at the Church' in a falsetto voice.

After that, Uncle Dick laid his violin down and got to his feet. The room went quiet. Uncle took a moment to adjust his jacket, straighten his tie and smooth his moustache.

He took a deep breath and launched into recitation after recitation. 'Dat Leetle Baptiste' by Robert Service was followed by 'The Wreck of the Julie Plante' and before anyone could ask for it, he moved on without missing a beat to everyone's favourite, 'The Cremation of Sam McGee'. He didn't mind at all when we chimed in here and there with the parts we remembered from his previous visits.

Then he took us across the sea, so to speak, and recited "We 'ave an aspidistra in the parlour' in a perfect Cockney accent.

We finished off with a sing-song that included 'Alouette, Gentille Alouette'[42] for the French Canadians among us, 'Danny Boy' for the Irish, 'My Bonnie Lies Over the Ocean' for the Scots, 'There'll Always Be an England' for the Brits and 'Yankee Doodle' out of respect for our neighbours to the south.

At the end, we clapped 'til our hands were sore. Uncle Dick bowed gallantly and put away his violin with a promise to come back next year. Mum and Mrs. Byrne went to make the tea while the ladies unpacked their shoeboxes and filled the waiting platters with sandwiches and cakes for everyone to enjoy.

Refreshed in body and spirit, we said our goodbyes and made our way

---

[42] Sparrow, nice sparrow

home. As we walked along, Uncle Dick studied the stars, pointing out the Big Dipper and Orion's Belt and rhyming off the distances between the earth and the planets. We held hands with him and hung on to his every word wishing the night would never end.

Uncle Dick—how we loved him!

Chapter 23

The Sweet Smells of Christmas

My sister and I have shared more than 70 Christmases but the one we remember the best is the one we spent in the country. Every detail remains etched in our minds like frost on a windowpane.

The year was 1957 and we had been invited by André and Huguette Poirier and their daughter, Sylvie, to spend Christmas with them on their farm a few miles from our summer home in Stonefield.

We set off late in the afternoon of December 24. As soon as we crossed the Perley Bridge from Hawkesbury to Grenville and turned onto Route 29 we were enchanted by the sight of the fields completely covered by a thick blanket of snow.

Lights twinkled from the windows of houses and the pungent smell of wood smoke hung in the air.

Sylvie and her Dad were waiting at the end of their driveway when we arrived, stamping their feet and swinging a lantern to light our way. We climbed out of the car and exchanged 'Bonjours'[43] and hugs. Madame Poirier was watching from the window. She flew to the door and called out, "Vite, vite. Entrez, entrez. C'est trop froid dehors!"[44]

The kitchen was warm and steamy and we felt right at home as we pulled our chairs close to the stove and sat down to enjoy a cup of tea and a good chin-wag. Madame Poirier had been cooking all day in preparation for the Réveillon[45] that would follow Midnight Mass and the delicious smell of pigs' feet, ragoût de boulettes[46] and tourtières [47]made our mouths water.

At 7 o'clock Madame Poirier served us a light supper of soup and home-made bread followed by doughnuts and more cups of tea. "Just a little something for now because we don't want to spoil our appetites for later, do we?"she asked.

At ten o'clock, Madame Poirier slid the big pots of pigs' feet and ragoût to the back of the stove to simmer and slipped some meat pies into the oven to warm up. She placed a beautifully frosted 'Bûche de Noel[48] in the center of the dining-room table and sprinkled a drift of icing sugar over the top. The table sparkled with her best dishes and cutlery and a pair of tall red candles stood guard over it all.

At eleven o'clock Madame Poirier said to us, "Our tradition is to go to Midnight Mass with the horse and sleigh. Dress up well because there's no heater in the sleigh, remember."

Monsieur Poirier and Dad went out to hitch Queenie to the sleigh while Sylvie, Diane and I went to get ready.

Diane was still buttoning her coat and I was just about to put on my scarf when Sylvie whispered, "Here, have a few drops of my 'Evening in Paris' cologne. All the boys of the parish will be in church. Some of them are really cute so the smell of this perfume will make them notice us for sure."

I dabbed a bit behind my ears and handed the bottle to Diane who did the same before giving it back to Sylvie.

"That won't get us anywhere," she scoffed and with that she shook the bottle hard, sending the entire contents cascading down both our necks and hers.

---

[43] Hellos

[44] Quick, quick. Come in, come in. It's too cold outside.

[45] Traditional celebration after mid-night on Christmas Eve

[46] Meat-ball stew

[47] Meat pies

[48] Christmas cake shaped like a log

"Now wrap your scarves tight around your necks. Maman[49] doesn't approve of wearing perfume to church so don't undo your scarves until I say so," she warned.

Monsieur Poirier was waiting for us beside the sleigh, his arms piled high with bearskin robes. Dad spread a couple of them on the seat and when we climbed in, he draped another one across our laps. It was as heavy as lead. The night air was freezing so we dragged the fur right up to our chins. Immediately we were overcome by a strong smell of—well – dead bears I guess. We gagged and held our noses and complained until a word from Madame Poirier shut us up.

"You can get out and walk if you prefer," she said sweetly, "It's only three miles to the church."

We didn't care for that solution, so we pushed the stinking fur away from our faces, pulled our scarves up over our noses and found blessed relief in the powerful fumes of 'Evening in Paris'.

Dad climbed up to sit beside Monsieur Poirier and Mum and Madame Poirier sat facing us three girls. Monsieur Poirier flicked the reins and Queenie broke into a steady trot, setting the bells on her harness jingling cheerily. Madame Poirier began to sing 'Vive le vent!'[50] and Sylvie, Diane, Mum and I joined in. Queenie tossed her head and swished her tail and the thud of her hoof beats echoed across the silent fields. As we drew closer to the church, the church bells began to clang, welcoming everyone to Midnight Mass.

In the churchyard, Monsieur Poirier hitched Queenie to the rail alongside several other horses and sleighs. He threw a thick woolen blanket across her back and attached a nose bag half-full of oats to her bridle.

"She's getting on in years," he explained as I stood watching, "and she feels the cold so the oats will warm her belly. She'll be full of pep for the ride home."

Inside the church, small votive candles flickered on every windowsill and large candelabras lit up the chancel. The organist played the opening chords of 'Minuit Chretien' and we stood to sing the soaring notes of the beautiful hymn.

Monsieur Le Curé[51], preceded by two dishy altar boys, entered the chancel.

---

[49] Mummy
[50] Long live the wind.
[51] Title of the priest

Sylvie elbowed Diane and me and hissed, "See what I mean? Ooh-la-la!

Monsieur Le Curé waved the censer and the sweet smell of incense wreathed around our heads. Sylvie, Diane and I kept our eyes glued to the altar boys while the Mass unfolded with great ceremony.

When Monsieur Le Curé announced that the next hymn was, 'Quelle est cette odeur agréable?' Sylvie nudged me and sniffed her scarf. Of course we couldn't help but giggle. We didn't laugh for long though because Madame Poirier gave us a fearsome frown and waggled her finger at us.

When it was time for Communion, Sylvie made sure we were in line well ahead of our parents and right between two groups of very handsome boys.

"Now!" she whispered to Diane and me. We unwound our scarves and moved as close as we could to the boys ahead of us without actually treading on their heels.

"C'est chaud ici, n'est-ce pas?"[52] Sylvie commented in a voice loud enough to wake the dead.

"Yes, it is hot," Diane agreed just as loudly. We flapped our scarves and sent waves of 'Evening in Paris' toward the boys. They looked back over their shoulders and held their noses.

Diane and I were crushed but Sylvie didn't miss a beat. She turned to face the boys behind us and pretended to be looking over their heads for her parents.

"Can you see Papa et Maman?[53]" she asked Diane and me archly.

We turned around and flapped our scarves. One boy sniffed loudly and promptly had a noisy coughing fit. The other one made a big show of taking out his handkerchief and covering his whole face with it. Diane and I were mortified but Sylvie took it all in stride.

"What can you expect?" she said loftily, "Most of the boys in this parish live on farms so all they've ever smelled is 'Eau de vache'[54]! They don't know a thing about French perfume."

Following Communion, Monsieur Le Curé intoned the final blessing and everyone streamed outside. Happy cries of 'Merry Christmas' and 'Joyeux Noel'[55] rang out all around.

Overhead, the church bells bonged out their message of peace and joy

---

[52] It's hot in here, isn't it?

[53] Dad and Mum

[54] Cow's water

[55] Merry Christmas

while the horses whinnied and snorted, eager to head home to the warmth of their stables and the sweet-smelling hay in their mangers.

Monsieur Poirier removed Queenie's nosebag and rubbed her neck.

"Did you enjoy your treat, old girl?" he asked. She bobbed her head as if to say yes and stamped her feet on the frozen ground.

We set off for the farm in a flurry of more good wishes. Overhead the stars sparkled in the dark sky like slivers of ice. A half-moon floated overhead adding a gentle glow to the heavens.

Monsieur Poirier held Queenie to a walk until we were out of the village but as soon as we turned into the road that led to the farm he slapped the reins on her rump and called out, "À la maison, Queenie, pis vite. C'est Noël!"[56]

The old horse broke into a thundering gallop. Snow flew up from her hooves and the bells on her harness bounced so hard I thought they'd fall off. Queenie kept tossing her head and snorting, sending clouds of steam into the air. She looked like she was enjoying herself.

Getting into the spirit of things, Sylvie and Diane and I threw off the smelly bearskin robes, jumped to our feet, threw our hats and scarves on the seat and began to sing at the top of our lungs, "Jingle Bells, jingle bells, jingle all the way, Faster, Queenie, faster. Oh what fun it is to ride in a one-horse open sleigh, Hey! Plus vite, Queenie, plus vite!"[57]

The old girl put her heart and soul into it, I must say. Sides heaving and mouth foaming, she tore up one hill and raced down the next. The snow was glistening, the stars were shining and we were having the time of our lives. Finally out of breath and hot from the exertion of singing, we flopped back on the seat to catch our breath.

"We're almost home," Madame Poirier said, "Is anyone hungry?"

"We're all starving," Diane shouted.

"I can smell the Ragoût de Boulettes from here," Dad yelled throwing his head back and taking a big sniff.

"I can smell the Tourtières," I bellowed pulling the freezing air deep into my lungs.

Monsieur Poirier roared, "I can smell the pigs' feet and I can't wait to eat a big plateful."

"Funny, I think I smell perfume," said Mum, sounding puzzled.

---

[56] Go home, Queenie and fast. It's Christmas.

[57] Faster, Queenie, faster.

At precisely that moment, Queenie lifted her tail and blasted us with a very loud and foul smelling F--er—um -well, it wasn't 'Evening in Paris'. Ah yes, the smells of Christmas, 1957, we remember them well.

Heaven

Every June for almost 20 years, our family packed our summer clothes in a big steamer trunk and traded the heat and noise of Montreal for the peace and quiet of the country. 449 Moffat Avenue stopped being our address the minute Dad unlocked the door of our blue and white clapboard house in Stonefield.

We had arrived in heaven.

For the next ten weeks I didn't think about the kids who lived on my street in the city or the games we played in the coal sheds and back lanes. I erased all thoughts of school from my mind and completely forgot about side-walks, paved roads, telephones, electric lights and running water.

I scampered up the stairs to bed and slid down the banister for breakfast. At night, I counted the stars through my bedroom window and fell asleep to the chirping of crickets. In the morning I woke to the chattering of chipmunks and the slow clip-clop of horses as they pulled the hay wagons to the fields.

The milk I drank was still warm from the cow and the berries I ate shimmered with dew. I pumped ice-cold water from the well and hunted for pearly mushrooms in the woods.

I lived in heaven.

I swam in the still water of the Grenville Canal and paddled my canoe in the churning rapids of the Ottawa River. The leafy forest was my thinking place and the stony fields were my playground. The people who lived round about me and on the surrounding farms were my friends. They were never too busy to talk for a while, and always had room for me at their table.

I was happy in heaven.

One day a stranger appeared in Stonefield.He parked his big black car, took out a shiny leather briefcase and strode through the village. He called on every family and argued with the men. He made the women cry and frightened the children. He left an official document and a cheque on every kitchen table, including ours.

When he drove away, Stonefield didn't feel like heaven any more.Through their tears my parents explained to me that people in the city needed more electricity to turn on their lights, play their radios and iron their clothes. They described how the government was going to build a dam in the Ottawa River about 10 miles downstream at Carillon, to provide that electric power.

They said that everyone in Stonefield would have to leave the houses and land that had sheltered and fed them for generations and start new lives in different places. We could never even come back for a visit because Stonefield was going to be swallowed up by the rising water that would eventually power the dam.

Suddenly Heaven was a scary place.

I watched, broken-hearted while our neighbours and friends packed up their belongings, loaded their animals onto trucks, and drove away. When it was our turn, we took only a few treasured items and left everything else behind. Dad didn't even lock the door.

I whispered good-bye to Heaven.

Slowly the river began to rise. The roaring rapids were drowned first. Then the water crept up over the river bank and smothered the stony beaches. All the little creatures fled as the water snaked its way into their holes and dens. The golden hayfields turned into glassy blue ponds and still the water kept rising. In the woods the stately maples and graceful elm trees drooped in despair. Gradually they lost their grip on the sodden earth and at last they fell.

Soon the water was lapping at the doorsills of the empty houses and barns. It seeped through foundations and flowed boldly through windows and doors. One by one the once strong buildings shuddered and collapsed. Even the chimneys and weather vanes disappeared from view. An oppressive silence rolled across the huge expanse of water.

All traces of Stonefield were gone.

Downstream at Carillon the giant turbines of the dam churned out their kilowatts and their megawatts and the people in the city rejoiced.

But I wept, because I used to live in Heaven.

Snippets from the porch

Did she ever have a husband?

Well, if she did, she must have bottled him,
'cause there was no funeral.

• • •

You must remember Mrs. Pearce. She didn't keep her tongue in her pocket. When
she had something to say, she said it
and to hang with the consequences.

• • •

I don't like visiting my Aunt Aggie. She serves me the same sandwich every time.
Hot tongue and cold shoulder.

• • •

Nice woman but she couldn't carry a tune if it had a handle on it.

• • •

He was such a shy man, he never said a word. But if there was a dance, there
he'd be, hoofing around the floor with the rest of us.

• • •

She warned him one last time to stay out of the hotel.
He got tight. She sold the car.

• • •

When that lightning bolt hit the roof, I thought I'd been sent for.

• • •

I'm not surprised he can't get his work done. He goes from one thing to another,
like a turkey following a grasshopper.

• • •

They were so poor, they didn't have a pot or a window.

• • •

We froze like carrots. You could have snapped us in half.

• • •

She's just like an old pine tree. Once she's down, she'll never get up.

• • •

She really shook his barley that time.

• • •

Myrtle Willett, nice lady, but a little short on grain.

• • •

Don't expect Fred to pay a round in the hotel.
He hangs on to a nickel so tight, the beaver squeaks.

• • •

You must remember Annie. She lived on the back road
alongside all her buggy cousins.

⁋ *Acknowledgements* ⅋

In his book, 'La's Orchestra Saves the World', Alexander McCall Smith wrote, "Go to any small village in the world, and see what they remember. Everything. It's all there – passed on like a precious piece of information, some secret imparted from one who knew to one who yearns to know. Taken good care of.'

I couldn't go back to Stonefield, but I was yearning to know, so I did the next best thing. I sought out long-lost friends and neighbours. I asked them if they would consider telling me what they remembered and if they would welcome my questions. They were just as quick to open their homes and their hearts to me as they had done for my parents many years ago. I thank them for every story they told me, every burst of laughter we shared and every tear that fell.

My sister, Diane and our friends, Ross and Cheryl also have a rich store of memories of our Stonefield days. When we get together, all that has to happen is for one of us to ask, 'Do you remember….' and the floodgates open. Our friend, Sylvia, who grew up near Stonefield can still surprise us with tales about people and happenings that we had either forgotten or never known. All of this affirms what Alexander McCall Smith wrote—'everything is there, ready to be passed on. All has been well taken care of.' I thank them for jogging my memory and for providing information that has added authenticity to my stories.

Thanks also to Mary Ellen Mueller Legault who coupled her artistic talent with intuition and imagination to produce all the illustrations in this book. She laid down her brushes and turned from painting beautiful water-colours of the French country-side to work in an entirely different medium. She took time to study every story and using pen and ink, captured the essence of each one. Her ability to bring characters to life is truly awe-inspiring. The whimsy of some of her drawings and the stark sadness of others reveal what an insightful and sympathetic person Mary Ellen is.

My son-in-law, Gordon Osborne used his photographic expertise to restore my precious but very-tattered photographs. His quiet determination and professional 'eye' recovered details that had faded out of sight and mind. I thank him not only for his work, but the sincere interest he took in each photograph.

I am very grateful to Louise Sproule who combined patience, enthusiasm and editorial wisdom with publishing know-how to bring this book to completion. Her support and encouragement are deeply appreciated. Louise's knowledge of local history and her respect for people and the events that have shaped their lives, affirmed for me that my stories are worth telling.

My husband Richard has been a constant and positive presence every step of the way. He has listened to me talk about Stonefield for over 50 years without a word of complaint. He happily accompanies me to the very edge

Acknowledgements

of the river where Stonefield once was, and has eaten many a picnic lunch perched on a rock while I describe the way things used to be. His unwavering encouragement and support have pulled me through times when I doubted myself. I thank him with all my heart.

A particular thank-you is owed to my daughters, Gabrielle and Valerie, who unwittingly put me on the path to becoming an author the night they put their big book of fairy tales back on the shelf and asked for a Stonefield story instead.

Thank-you to all my students who taught me that time telling stories is time well-spent. Their comments and questions pointed out the strengths and the weaknesses of my tales and pushed me to search for the right words and the most descriptive phrases possible.

Special mention must be made of the late Leonard Dupuis. He was an invaluable source of information for my stories but more importantly, he was an inspiration. Leonard only lived in Stonefield for the first few years of his life but his family made sure that he grew up well-versed in the history of his own people in particular, and the history of Stonefield in general. His detailed accounts of the quiet routines and unexpected complications of country life enthralled me and to my great delight, he peppered these accounts with amusing asides and colourful expressions that often left me weak with laughter. His love for Stonefield shone through every anecdote he shared and revealed the same longing to go 'home' that I still feel today. He was taken from us unexpectedly and much too soon. I deeply regret that he is not here to hold my book in his hand.